McKINLEY, BRYAN, AND THE PEOPLE

McKinley, Bryan, and the People

By PAUL W. GLAD

ELEPHANT PAPERBACKS
Ivan R. Dee, Publisher, Chicago

First ELEPHANT PAPERBACK edition published 1991 by Ivan R. Dee, Inc., 1332 North Halsted Street, Chicago 60622. Manufactured in the United States of America and printed on acid-free paper.

Library of Congress Cataloging-in-Publication Data:
Glad, Paul W., 1926–
McKinley, Bryan, and the people / by Paul W. Glad. — 1st elephant paperback ed.
p. cm.
Reprint. Originally published: Philadelphia : Lippincott, 1964.
Includes bibliographical references and index.
ISBN 0-929587-49-9 (acid-free paper)
1. Presidents—United States—Election—1896. 2. United States—Politics and government—1893–1897. 3. McKinley, William, 1843–1901. 4. Bryan, William Jennings, 1860–1925. I. Title.
E710.G55 1991
324.973′087—dc20 90-47152

For Carolyn

Acknowledgments

MANY people have helped to write this book, and I wish to thank them for their assistance. I am under heavy obligation to Professor Charles Kendrick Cannon, a colleague at Coe College, for his judicious reading of the entire manuscript and for his many valuable recommendations. Professor Frank Otto Gatell of the University of Maryland read the first five chapters with infinite care and helped me to eliminate infelicities of style and weaknesses in presentation. Professor Ernest Isaacs of the University of Maryland and Professor Norman Charles of Pennsylvania State College, Millersville, made several key criticisms which sharpened my interpretation of men and events. Dr. Hans-Ulrich Wehler of the University of Cologne, Germany, made important suggestions on the relationship between economic developments and international relations in the 1890's. Professor Vincent De Santis of the University of Notre Dame read the manuscript in its entirety. I am grateful to Professor Samuel T. McSeveney, Los Angeles State College, for loaning me a copy of his provocative paper, "The Politics of Depression: Popular Voting Behavior, 1893-1896," which was read at the meeting of the Mississippi Valley Historical Association in the spring of 1961. I must also thank the many librarians—especially those associated with the Library of Congress, the Library of the State University of Iowa, and the Library of Coe College—for their help in locating materials relevant to the election of 1896. Finally, I acknowledge my deepest indebtedness to my wife, Carolyn Biede Glad, whose patience I must have strained, and upon whose judgment I have placed unlimited reliance.

Contents

McKINLEY, BRYAN, AND THE PEOPLE

I

OF MYTHS AND MEN

IN NOVEMBER, 1916, SHERWOOD ANDERSON, A BUSINESSman turned author, posted a letter to Waldo Frank, editor of *The Seven Arts Magazine.* "I made last year a series of intensive studies of people of my home town," he wrote. "In the book I called the town Winesburg, Ohio. Some of the studies you may think pretty raw and there is a sad note running through them. One or two of them get pretty closely down to the ugly things of life." Anderson went on to add that these studies "will suggest the real environment out of which present day American youth is coming."

What was remarkable in Anderson's comments was not the observation that American youth was leaving the rural village; that movement had been going on for some time. What was remarkable was the author's attitude toward the village. The country town contained for him and for others of his literary generation some of the ugliest things of life. It was raw, mean, stagnant, and hypocritical. Americans had not always seen the rural community in this light. In the post-Civil War period, even as urbanization proceeded at a rapid rate, the country town occupied an important place in American mythology. Closely identified with the Jeffersonian tradition of yeoman simplicity, it was widely regarded as the font of goodness and the conservator of moral values.

At the same time, as a new urban, industrial society challenged older rural values, another myth began to bulk large in the popular mind. This was the myth of the self-made man, which for a century or more had run parallel to the myth of rural virtue. During the gilded age captains of industry gloried in the idea that, as Andrew Carnegie put it, "the millionaires who are in active control started as poor boys and were trained in the sternest but most efficient of all schools—poverty." That notion did not precisely correspond to the facts, but it was nonetheless prevalent.

The two myths, distinct and separate, would at times complement each other. Horatio Alger neatly wove the two together in his best-selling tales of poor boys who made good. He almost invariably supplied his heroes with rural or small-town origins, as if to say that strength of character could best be developed in the country. On the other hand, it was in the city with its manifold opportunities that his impeccable little messengers and venders rose to the top. One of the reasons Abraham Lincoln became an important symbol in the period when schoolboys were reading the Alger books was that he, too, embodied both themes; he was a country boy and a self-made man.

As a rule, however, politicians were never so closely associated with the myth of the self-made man as they were with the myth of rural virtue. The reason is quite simple. Politicians were seldom millionaires and could not, therefore, offer what in that age was the most dramatic proof of an open-class system. But like most Americans, they had direct or indirect rural connections, and in appeals for farm votes they made the most of them. All the solemn, bearded presidents who followed Lincoln could boast of agrarian or small-town antecedents. Most of them were from the Middle West, or at least had had careers west of the Alleghenies. At a time when many of the best minds in the nation sought the stimulation of cosmopolitan universities in Europe and America, they either studied independently or breathed the moral-intellectual atmosphere of small liberal arts colleges: Hayes went to Kenyon College, Garfield to Hiram and to Williams, Arthur to Union, and Harrison to Miami

University. All except Grant and Garfield read and practiced law, but only Arthur sought a career in the city. They were solid, substantial men, and they did not come from a privileged class. But they were not self-made men. Their advancement resulted not from native business shrewdness, but from success at the polls. A Carnegie or a Rockefeller could apparently stand alone without fear or favor; the bearded presidents were indebted to voters and to campaign contributors.

The society that elected those men to high office was the society in which William McKinley and William Jennings Bryan grew to political maturity. Neither one rebelled against the dominant beliefs and values of his time and place. Both were born and reared in the Middle West. Both received their education there; Bryan studied four years at Illinois College, while McKinley was a student at Allegheny College for less than a year. Both were steeped in the moralistic tradition of American Protestantism. Both entered the legal profession, thereby rejecting careers in business in order to further political ambitions.

While the two men had much in common they differed, however, in some critical respects. McKinley's outstanding Civil War record was a decided political asset; Bryan, who was only five years old when Lee surrendered to Grant, was an attractive figure because of his youthful vigor. But more important, McKinley was a Republican and Bryan was a Democrat. Differences in age and family background help to account for differences in party affiliation. Yet McKinley was as convinced that the Republican party could best serve the nation as Bryan was that Democratic leadership was essential. In the twenty years after 1876 the central issue dividing the two parties was the tariff, and on that issue Bryan and McKinley held opposite views. Bryan consistently urged the Democratic position of "tariff for revenue only," while McKinley championed a policy of protection.

Whatever its economic significance, the tariff question was important because it suggested the essential difference between the two men who were to become protagonists in the drama of 1896.

Support of the protective tariff, in the popular mind, meant creating new opportunities for businessmen. It was a legislative extension of the myth of the self-made man. On the other side, opposition to the tariff was natural for one who identified himself with the rural elements in American society. McKinley, whose financial ventures revealed no great business insight, accepted completely the outlook of the captain of industry. Bryan, whose business transactions indicate considerable understanding of such matters, adhered to the point of view of the farmer. The difference between Bryan and McKinley was more one of degree and of emphasis than of kind. Without turning his back on the myth of rural virtue—to do so would have meant political suicide—McKinley made the myth of the self-made man the rationale for his program. Bryan, a firm believer in the simple virtues of the yeoman, insisted that the farmers were businessmen too and that they were being denied opportunities to advance on the ladder of economic success.

William McKinley, Jr., was born in 1843 in the hamlet of Niles, Ohio, where his father struggled to obtain a livelihood from a small charcoal furnace. It was no easy task, for there were nine children in the McKinley family. The father was as diligent and industrious as his Scotch-Irish and English Puritan ancestors, and just as poor. He and his wife were, however, ambitious for their children; if they could not provide physical comforts, they could and did take pains to provide educational advantages which they themselves had not enjoyed. Thus in 1852 the family moved to Poland, near Youngstown, so that the younger children could attend high school.

At Poland Academy young William was a plodder, an earnest student but not a brilliant one. Although he did not take part in games and sports, he did excel in public speaking. He was soon active in the debating societies which flourished there as they did in even the most provincial of middle western communities. Much to the satisfaction of his mother, he also participated in religious affairs. Shortly after the move to Poland he made a public profession of faith at a revival meeting, and when he was sixteen he became a member of the Methodist Church.

At this point in his life McKinley seemed destined for the ministry. To prepare for that calling he was sent to Allegheny College at Meadville, Pennsylvania. The few months during which he attended classes were critical ones for the nation; Lincoln was elected by a minority of the American people, and wherever two or three men gathered together, there was talk of secession and the possibility of war. Those months were critical for the McKinley family, too. William took sick at the end of his first term, and his father experienced financial difficulties which made a return to college out of the question. In the best self-made man tradition the youth went to work teaching school and clerking in the post office, hoping to accumulate enough money to continue his studies.

When Fort Sumter fell, war rallies were held all over the North. After attending one of them, William McKinley enlisted in the Union cause for three months or the duration. He remained in the army for four years. McKinley turned out to be an unusually good soldier, accepting without complaint the inconveniences of the camp, the rigors of forced marches, and the perils of battle. Much has been written about McKinley's spinelessness and moral cowardice after he became President. If he was indeed a moral coward (and it must be said that the charge is unfair), no one could deny his physical courage. He more than once proved himself in trials by combat.

On the monument-strewn field by Antietam Creek stands a memorial describing how commissary sergeant McKinley drove a mule team into the thick of the fighting carrying hot food and coffee to the troops. Visitors on reading of the incident might smile derisively; it seems such a trivial contribution to what some historians have thought the most important of Union victories. It might be observed, however, that the sergeant was under no compulsion to risk his life. He did so out of a powerful desire to help as best he could. It was as much in character for McKinley to perform his exploit as it was for the home folks in Ohio to celebrate it. As they read newspaper recapitulations of the battle, the young sergeant did not scruple to have his role called to the attention of the right people. His recent biographer, Margaret Leech, notes that this, too, was in character, for "he did not undervalue himself, and he never saw any harm in asking a favor in a nice, indirect way." In any case, Rutherford B. Hayes, commander of the regiment, wrote a letter of recommendation to the Governor of Ohio, and before long McKinley was sporting the bars of a second lieutenant.

McKinley served with distinction, first as aide-de-camp for Hayes and then as a staff officer for various generals, throughout the remainder of the war. *The Official Records of the Rebellion* mention his conduct at Opequan and his gallantry at Winchester. He received promotions periodically in recognition of his abilities and his bravery, and in 1865 he was mustered out with the brevet commission of major. He had seriously considered remaining in the army, but his family opposed the idea. He turned instead to the study of law which would fit him for a career in politics.

McKinley's former commanding officer, Hayes, had advised him to go into railroading or some other commercial activity. "A man in any of our Western towns with half your wit," he wrote, "ought to be independent at forty in business." But the law had its compelling attractions. Reading privately for a time, McKinley spent a term in law school at Albany, New York, with the financial help of his older sister, Anna. After passing his examinations and gaining entrance to the bar, he went to Canton, county seat of Stark County, Ohio. There he formed a fortunate partnership with an elderly judge who died leaving McKinley a well-established practice. As a lawyer he was successful for the same reasons he had been successful at Poland Academy and in the army. He was painstaking and hard-working. He expressed himself in cliché-ridden periods, but he was able to plead a case in terms that any jury could understand.

The Major was no back-slapping booster for Canton. Yet he did take part in many community affairs and was recognized by the citizenry as having a productive career ahead of him. He was aware of a lack of sophistication in himself; others found him distant and reserved. This did not, however, prevent him from joining organizations he thought worthwhile. He was a member of the Grand Army of the Republic and the Loyal Legion. He had become a Mason during the war, and he quickly affiliated with the local lodge. He joined the Knights of Pythias; he was active in the work of the YMCA. He faithfully attended the services of the Methodist Church and was soon made superintendent of the Sunday School. His willingness to assume obligations, his avoidance of frivolities such as dancing and card playing, and his refusal to associate with the hard-drinking habitués of the livery stable and the saloon earned him the respect of the best people. Yet there was nothing of the snob in McKinley's makeup. Laborers of Stark County cherished a warm feeling for him after he refused payment for defending a group of Massillon miners imprisoned for riot during a strike.

Almost immediately after his move to Canton, McKinley became involved in politics. He worked hard to carry Stark County for Hayes in the gubernatorial campaign of 1867, and his efforts were successful even though the county was normally Democratic. The next year he became still more active in Grant's presidential campaign. McKinley himself ran for prosecuting attorney and won in a Republican landslide. By 1876, having served his apprenticeship, he was ready to run for Congress. Again he was successful, and he began a long—though not unbroken—tenure in the House of Representatives that was to last until 1890. His chief problem in the elections of those years was with the Ohio legislature. When the Democrats secured a majority, they gerrymandered his district, and McKinley had to fight to hold his office. Yet he continued to win. In 1882, when his plurality was only eight votes out of 33,000, he was unseated by a Democratic House. But not until 1890, when he was faced with the third gerrymander of his district and with opposition to the legislation of the Republican Fifty-first Congress, was he actually defeated at the polls. Although he never again ran for his old seat in the House, McKinley rejected any thought of retiring from politics. He received the Republican nomination for governor in 1891, and he returned to his winning ways. He was re-elected in 1893 with a thumping majority.

More than anything else vote getting commands the respect of professional politicians. McKinley's record could not be ignored, and steadily he rose to prominence in his party. In 1880 he was temporary chairman of the Ohio Republican convention. That same year, after Garfield's nomination, he won a place on the all important Ways and Means Committee where he was to make a national reputation as his party's chief advocate of a protective tariff. He was still little known to the country in 1884, although he served as permanent chairman of the Ohio convention and as a member of the resolutions committee of the national Republican convention. When Congress convened in December, 1889, McKinley was a candidate for the House speakership. He lost that position to astute, caustic Thomas B. Reed of Maine, but he hid his disappointment in the interests of party harmony and was rewarded with the chairmanship of the Ways and Means Committee. He was thus responsible for introducing the tariff with which his name became associated. In 1892 the now famous Governor of Ohio was permanent chairman of the national party convention in Minneapolis.

It could not be said that McKinley ever appeared unduly ambitious for place and prestige. If he sought promotion within party ranks, it was never with Machiavellian cunning. The character of the man was well revealed in the infighting at the convention of 1888. McKinley was pledged to his fellow Ohioan, the Mr. Republican of his day, Senator John Sherman. The weakness of the Sherman candidacy soon appeared in the balloting, however, and there were rumors that another Ohio man would stand a better chance to get his name on the national ticket. McKinley, who would certainly have been a logical choice for vice president if not for president, refused to make any deals. With some passion he addressed the delegates, demanding that no votes be cast for him and affirming his loyalty to Sherman.

McKinley's evident sense of honor, his insistence on sticking by his word, and his devotion to his party won him many friends in 1888. None was to be more important to him than Mark Hanna, a no-nonsense Ohio capitalist who had also supported Sherman. Hanna could appreciate honor and loyalty when he saw it, and he was ready to use his considerable wealth in the interest of just such a man as McKinley. Thus without taking the initiative himself, the Major received support from one of the shrewdest, most canny politicians of his time.

Hanna traveled to Washington in 1889 to help in McKinley's quest for the House speakership. Though he failed in that endeavor, his influence was doubtless important in securing the chairmanship of the Ways and Means Committee for his new friend. Later, he moved quietly in the background of McKinley's gubernatorial campaign, visiting manufacturers and suggesting how they might express their gratitude to the author of the 1890 tariff act. At the party conclave in 1892 Hanna was ready to press for McKinley should the delegates rebel against renominating Harrison, a possibility that was not unlikely since the crusty old President had alienated many a GOP leader. Hanna set up unofficial headquarters in Minneapolis and had some heart-to-heart talks with members of the Republican Sanhedrin. As in 1888, however, McKinley's pronouncements were politically impeccable. He took little notice of Hanna's efforts and insisted that Harrison had every right to a renomination. When the convention adjourned, its permanent chairman could not have been in a better position. The Republican outlook was far from brilliant in 1892, but McKinley would not be blamed for the party's defeat. He had emerged as the most popular man at the convention and the most widely discussed possibility for the nomination in 1896. After the election Hanna and the Governor would set to work formulating long-range plans.

McKinley's remarkable achievements at the polls, his growing prominence within the Republican party, and the shrewdness of Mark Hanna do not in themselves explain the ultimate success of those plans. What was there about McKinley that could account for his political popularity? Why did he become such an attractive possibility in 1896?

McKinley was not born under a lucky star. Endowed with modest talents, he made his way with diligent application and hard work. According to the code by which he lived, serenity of mind and personal happiness almost always resulted from honorable enterprise. Yet McKinley's life was not a happy one. It should have been—it gave every promise of being—joyous and satisfying. As a young lawyer in Canton the Major had married vivacious Ida Saxton, daughter of one of the town's leading bankers and businessmen

Within a year the couple announced the birth of a daughter, Katherine. A few months later the Major and his wife, awaiting the arrival of a second child, experienced a series of crises that would shatter their happiness forever. It began with the death of Mrs. Saxton. The young wife underwent labor in a state of extreme grief for her mother, and there were complications. The infant lived less than five months; Ida herself never recovered. Her subsequent periodic convulsions indicated some damage to the brain, and phlebitis crippled her so that she moved about with the greatest difficulty. Then little Katie died in 1876 at the age of four.

William McKinley was not Job. No one told him to curse God and die. No one advised him to look for the sin that had brought all his suffering. No one would ever know what questions he raised with himself during those dark hours; certainly he did not doubt the righteousness and justice of God. When the worst was over, he nursed his wife with tact and patience, always hopeful that she would recover. At the same time he threw himself into political discussions, political campaigns, political strategy, political problems with irrepressible energy. Politics was not a game for McKinley; it was his life. Politics provided release from domestic care and anxiety and gave him a sense of fulfillment.

McKinley never asked for the sympathy which a sentimental age was all too ready to give. He seldom mentioned his personal problems, and he never played the role of a martyr. He always maintained a certain reserve; the thought that he could use his wife's illness to good political purpose would have appalled him. Yet McKinley suffered much. And his own sorrow helped to bring out the compassion and kindliness that were deeply imbedded in his character. He had, in short, a warm human touch that won the love of his colleagues and—it sounds harsh to say it—votes.

Not that McKinley was always fully understood or appreciated. He had been successful in Ohio politics, remarked the usually perceptive William Allen White, "where survival values combined the virtues of the serpent, the shark, and the cooing dove." But for White's taste too much of the cooing dove predominated. McKinley, he explained, "used too many hackneyed phrases, too many stereotyped forms. He shook hands with exactly the amount of cordiality and with precisely the lack of intimacy that deceived men into thinking well of him, too well of him." Then shifting the scene from the jungle to the pharmacy, White wrote, "He weighed out his saccharine on apothecary scales, just enough and no more for the dose that cheers but does not inebriate." While those who opposed McKinley might agree with this evaluation (might even put it more strongly than Republican White), his friends and supporters regarded him as wise in a down-to-earth, practical way. In the alliterative phrase so commonly applied, he was "safe and sane." To this, McKinley's opponents would counter that he was indeed safe for special interests because he was a kept man. In the caricatures of Homer Davenport, cartoonist of the New York *Journal*, Mark Hanna became the symbol of bloated plutocracy pulling the strings of puppet McKinley.

Most of these impressions and assessments were wide of the mark. White made McKinley appear more canting and disingenuous than he actually was. He made bromidic speeches, not because he wished to drug his listeners, but because he actually believed his hackneyed phrases embodied the highest truth. Hardheaded businessmen supported him, not because he was one of them, but because his views on the tariff and other economic questions coincided with their own. The suggestion that McKinley had sold his soul to corporate interests failed to account for personal experience. "The duty on foreign iron had not been an abstract idea to an ironfounder's son," writes Margaret Leech, "but the source of bread and butter, and the memories of want rang in McKinley's phrases when he spoke of the low tariff years of his boyhood."

In truth McKinley was a simple man who had neither the inclination nor the imagination to probe deeply into theoretical questions. He was not reflective enough to see that personal experience, his own and that of others, was not always a reliable guide. "I would rather have my political economy founded upon the everyday experience of the puddler or the potter than the learning of the professor," he once wrote. Yet his benevolent simplicity and his banality are only a part of the truth about McKinley. Within limits imposed by his experience and by the myths which governed his thought, he did have his areas of special competence. Earlier than most of his contemporaries he saw the relationship between foreign trade and development of the American economy. Of more immediate importance, he understood the practical side of American politics as well as anyone has ever understood it. That understanding would serve him well in the crucial conflict that lay ahead.

In the closing hours of his third presidential campaign in 1908, William Jennings Bryan spoke in his neighborly way to the people of Lincoln, Nebraska:

> I have been the child of fortune from my birth. God gave me into the keeping of a Christian father and a Christian mother. They implanted in my heart the ideals that have guided my life. When I was in law school, I was fortunate enough, as I was in my college days, to fall under the influence of men of ideals who helped to shape my course; and when but a young man, not out of college yet, I was guided to the selection of one who, for twenty-four years, has been my faithful helpmate.

The influences Bryan mentioned in 1908 were just as real in 1896. McKinley experienced domestic misfortunes that Bryan would never know. Bryan enjoyed educational opportunities that were denied McKinley. Much of McKinley's time and thought was taken up with political tactics and strategy. Bryan, himself no mean tactician in party and intraparty battles, was perhaps more interested in preaching the ideals implanted in his heart.

Bryan was born in Salem, Illinois, in 1860. He grew up in a household in which religious observances were given an important place. His Baptist father, Silas Bryan, never wavered in his loyalty to his church. His mother, Mariah Jennings Bryan, was more emotional, but just as committed to her faith. During the week Mariah might sing to her children the sentimental ballads of the Civil War years, but on Sunday afternoons the family would gather about the piano to sing hymns. (Silas Bryan's favorite: "Kind Words Can Never Die.") The elder Bryan was always more interested in moral instruction than in theology, and he often read aloud from the Book of Proverbs. Those hours of family fellowship were also occasions for poetry reading and discussion of edifying topics. They provided inspiration for the daily lessons in reading and writing which Mariah gave her small children.

Silas Bryan was never a man plagued with doubt. The solidity of his political convictions matched that of his religious ideas, and it brought him some measure of political success. Originally a Jacksonian Democrat, he served eight years in the Illinois state senate, was twice elected a state judge, and was a member of the Illinois Constitutional Convention of 1869. The controversy over slavery and the Civil War brought changes in his affiliations but not in his opinions. Supported by the Greenback party, he ran unsuccessfully for Congress in 1872. The austere judge believed firmly in expanded currency, in keeping the powers of government to a minimum, and in equal opportunities for all.

By the mid-nineteenth century standards of southern Illinois, the Bryans lived well. Theirs was a large house just outside the village of Salem, and young Willy took to the bucolic environment in which he was reared. Later in life he recalled the pleasure with which he had hunted rabbits in the fields around the Bryan property. Yet he never became a sportsman. His only athletic distinction was his skill in broad jumping and in jumping backwards, which, strangely enough, none of his detractors ever seemed to find symbolically significant.

Judge Bryan was not accustomed to wasting his substance, yet he indulged in one excess on his acreage: a deer park. Despite his Jacksonian persuasion, he occasionally displayed a hankering for aristocratic ways. For a time he talked of sending William to Oxford, but in the end rejected the idea. The elder Bryan did, after all, take a democratic view of education. Learning was valuable, not for its own sake, or even for the prestige it might confer. It was valuable because it provided opportunities. And in any case, the family decided, an education second to none was available close at hand. So William packed his bags and went to live with a distant relative, Dr. Hiram K. Jones, in Jacksonville, where he spent six years attending Whipple Academy and Illinois College.

The high opinion which the Bryans held of Jacksonville as a center of intellectual activity should not be dismissed out of hand as a bumpkin delusion. The community, unlike some others in the West, had since frontier days sought to encourage the life of the mind. In addition to Whipple Academy and Illinois College, it was the location of Jacksonville Female Academy, Illinois Women's College, and state schools for the deaf and the blind. Perhaps even more significant were the clubs and discussion groups which flourished there. The most important of them were the two in which Dr. Jones was a moving spirit, the Plato Club and its successor the American Akademe. These were made up largely of amateur philosophers, but there are few hints of Babbittry in their objectives. They were seeking metaphysical frames of reference to encompass everyday problems, and Dr. Jones contributed much to such investigation. After his association with William Torrey Harris, Bronson Alcott, and Ralph Waldo Emerson in the Concord School of Philosophy, his reputation extended far beyond central Illinois.

Like almost every small liberal arts college in the West, Illinois had its limitations. The effort to locate a college at almost every crossroads inevitably meant that many of them would be faced with a constant struggle for survival. Illinois fared better than most, though to the eight men who made up the faculty in Bryan's day, financial difficulties must have seemed overwhelming. Whatever its shortcomings—in library resources, in classroom facilities, in staff—the College served Bryan well. It did not mold him into a scholar nor greatly challenge his intellect. But it did encourage him to think about what he should do with his life. It did give him resources to view his ideals in some perspective and opportunities to develop his talents.

Like McKinley, Bryan studied diligently; though he dazzled no one with his brilliance, he was valedictorian of the class of 1881. It was outside the classroom that he was most impressive. He became a member of Sigma Pi, the older of two literary societies, and he soon earned a reputation as an orator and debater. In the class poem of 1881, he received a typical nineteenth-century accolade:

Accustomed to dispute, with all compete,
He's learned to act in victory or defeat.
To eulogize in these degenerate days,
Would not enhance, but only mar one's praise.
The Fawns may flatter, Satyrs rage,
But merit proves itself in every age.

By his own account, Bryan's first ambition was to be a Baptist preacher, but a fear of baptism by immersion induced him to change his mind. At the time of his graduation, the Illinois *College Rambler*, a student publication, noted: "Law and politics are his friends, and he intends to court them as soon as other things will permit." What the "other things" might have been is not clear. Bryan certainly wasted no time, for within a few weeks he was in Chicago courting the law.

He spent two years there studying at the Union College of Law and reading in the office of Lyman Trumbull. The veteran lawyer had been in politics since his move to Illinois in 1836. Beginning in 1854 he had served three terms as United States senator and had taken a prominent part in the debates of the period. His political convictions had led him from one political camp to another. At first a Democrat, he had joined the Republicans and had associated himself with the radical faction of the party. Yet he had opposed the impeachment of President Johnson and ultimately had returned to the Democracy in 1876. Still dissatisfied, he had been active in the Greenback and other reform movements. When Bryan later recalled the men who had been influential in his life, he invariably mentioned Trumbull. Yet the influence was personal rather than ideological. More important to Bryan than Trumbull's principles was the fact that he had principles.

After passing his bar examinations, the young man returned to Jacksonville, the scene of earlier triumphs. He married Mary Baird, whom he had met when she was a student at Jacksonville Female Academy and he still a student at Illinois. Mamie was able and intelligent. (She studied law under her husband's guidance and was ultimately admitted to the bar in her own right.) Together they set up housekeeping and confidently awaited continuing success. They were disappointed. Bryan was by no means a failure as a lawyer, but for five years he was preoccupied with the more menial tasks of his profession—bill collecting and the like. The prize-winning college orator, who had never made any secret of his large ambitions and great expectations, could hardly rest content. Then, fortuitously, he made a trip west and stopped off in Lincoln, Nebraska, to visit a college friend. All prospects pleased, and with little persuasion Bryan decided to move. The days of marking time were at an end.

Bryan formed a partnership with his friend, A. R. Talbot, and he became active in the life of Lincoln. But it was politics, not the law or community affairs, that soon claimed his almost undivided attention. Old leaders of the state Democratic organization, men such as J. Sterling Morton and Dr. George L. Miller, found his oratorical skill a great boon in their efforts to build up the strength of the party. Bryan, for his part, was only too happy to oblige them by speaking whenever occasion offered. And opportunities to speak came with increasing frequency as his reputation grew.

The topic that most interested Bryan during his first years on the plains was also the topic to which William McKinley was particularly attracted. While McKinley labored on his tariff bill in the House of Representatives, Bryan was arguing against the principle of protection in Nebraska. By 1890 the Omaha *World Herald* was suggesting that "the young tariff orator of Lincoln" would be a logical choice for congressman from Nebraska's first district. When the district convention nominated him, the paper became rhapsodic: "Young, eloquent, earnest, and able, Bryan is the very best standard bearer who could have been chosen to lead the recently aroused masses against the fortifications behind which the favored classes are entrenched."

A practiced public speaker, Bryan knew how to make his points clear to the most obtuse of his listeners without insulting the most clever. In a political debate he was quick to find the weakness in his opponent's argument and quick to take advantage of it. His thrusts were swift and devastating. In prepared speeches his reasoning had a logical symmetry about it. He employed analogies with great effect, and his best orations were studded with allusions both homely and classical. He said, for example, speaking on the tariff:

> When Ulysses, returning home, approached the island of the sirens he put wax in the ears of his sailors and had himself tied to the ship's mast so he could not turn aside. We have no sirens singing today, but there is a voice of moaning coming up from the agricultural classes—a great wail of distress, and the commanders of the republican ship have stopped the ears of their sailors and made them deaf to the cry of the people, while they themselves are so tied to the protected interests by ante-election promises that hearing they cannot heed.

During his 1890 campaign Bryan emphasized the tariff more than any other question. He delivered over eighty speeches on the subject. Yet the tariff was not the only issue of the campaign. His opponents later asserted that Bryan won because he sold out to the liquor interests. This was a strange charge to make against a man who never drank anything stronger than sarsaparilla. It was based on the fact that he went along with his party in opposing a prohibition amendment to the state constitution. Instead of outright prohibition, Bryan and the Nebraska Democracy urged high license fees and local option. No doubt the wet vote did help to elect him, but it is clear that Bryan considered other factors more important.

His platform dealt with a variety of issues: the extravagance of the Republican Fifty-first Congress, the evils of subsidies and bounties, the desirability of reclaiming alien land holdings, the importance of having senators elected directly by the people, and reform of the House rules. The plank that was to have the greatest significance in his future was one calling for the "free coinage of silver on equal terms with gold." In 1890, however, Bryan was not yet ready to make the silver question paramount.

Taking his seat in the House of Representatives, from which McKinley had just been retired by the voters, the young Nebraskan secured appointment to the Ways and Means Committee, where McKinley had made such a name for himself. Bryan was thus placed in a position of unusual strategic importance for one so new in the House, and he made the most of it. He worked hard for tariff reform, but increasingly he became convinced that currency reform was even more vital. By 1892 he had become so partisan to the silver cause that he hoped the Democratic party would nominate Iowa silverite Horace Boies. The nomination and the election went instead to Grover Cleveland. Bryan, re-elected by a narrow margin, found himself in an awkward position during his second term. He could agree with Cleveland's tariff views, but he could not go along with the President's hard-money policy.

The inevitable result of that disagreement was a feud between Bryan and the conservative Democrats who supported Cleveland. The President was persuaded to withdraw all patronage, and for a time it looked as though he would be rid of the troublesome young orator from the plains. Nebraska Bourbons succeeded in preventing the state legislature from naming him United States senator in 1893 and again in 1895. The opposition to him was so strong that he did not even try to retain his seat in the House in 1894. But Bryan's difficulties with Cleveland Democrats did not mean that he could be counted out. Diligently he set about achieving two objectives: first, he sought to gain control of the party organization in Nebraska, and second, he worked to win a national following. With consummate skill he built his combinations.

Facile as he was in debate and clever as he was in advancing his cause, Bryan's thought was bounded by certain limits. The point of view he brought to every issue was one that had been shaped in Salem, in Jacksonville, and on the plains of Nebraska. Always a moralist, he saw political contests as not merely struggles for power but as struggles between good and evil. Always a Jeffersonian, he placed unbounded confidence in the views of the people. Always a Jacksonian, he steadfastly opposed privilege and monopoly. Always an agrarian, he expressed the opinions of his rural constituents. Given those predilections, his position on any specific question was almost always predictable. The protective tariff was not just economically misguided; it was morally wrong because it in effect took property from one and gave it to another. It benefited manufacturers and hurt farmers. It meant the accumulation of wealth, the corruption of legislators, and the growth of trusts and monopolies. The depression of the nineties, to Bryan's way of thinking, made the monetary question paramount. He looked to free silver—the money of the people—to right ancient wrongs. That the money question divided the party was unfortunate. Yet, as Bryan wrote one of his supporters, "to have ignored it without a protest would have been much worse."

Perhaps the fundamental point to be emphasized in any comparison of Bryan and McKinley is that both men were essentially conservative. In every personal quality the two reflected their respective portion of the American experience. In every expression of opinion, in every decision, and in every commitment, one could appeal to a tradition as characteristically American as could the other. It is true that in the dramatic campaign of 1896 Bryan became associated with agrarian radicalism. But that radicalism was by no means Marxist, and Bryan was certainly no Lenin. He did not look to the creation of a new society, but to the past for guidance in developing ways to meet new problems. He idealized the sturdy yeoman farmer of the Jeffersonian heritage, and he believed that without thwarting the development of industry, opportunities could still be provided for farmers and for all those who labored with their hands.

II

MYTHS AND REALITIES

WILLIAM JENNINGS BRYAN, DESPITE EPITHETS HURLED at him by his opponents, was not of the stuff of which revolutionaries are made. His was a mentality that found perfect satisfaction in the thought patterns of the Middle West in which he had been reared. The values and ideals he held dear were the values and ideals of his parents, his teachers, and his neighbors. He believed in the existence of a moral law and in the capacity of man to grow in his understanding of that moral law. He had no doubt that society would progress as moral principles, better understood, were more perfectly applied. He always assumed that of all groups and classes farmers were in the best position to grow in their understanding of the moral law. It went without saying—though of course Bryan said it anyway—that the American economy rested on rural foundations; farmers fed and therefore supported their fellow citizens in the cities. But in a peculiar way agriculture was important in a moral as well as in an economic sense. Living in close contact with nature, the sturdy yeoman developed into a particularly wholesome specimen. He was God's partner in the process of creation. He planted and God gave the increase. All honest occupations were honorable, but the farmer's virtue was conspicuous and his wisdom real.

Bryan thus accepted heart and soul the agrarian myth which had been a familiar configuration in the American mind for more than a century. That myth was not a distinctively American invention, nor did it develop first among small farmers. Its first promulgators on both sides of the Atlantic were the eighteenth-century gentry, the owners of large country estates. They themselves did not till the soil, for that task was performed by others. Their own managerial functions allowed them the leisure necessary for study and contemplation out of which a rationale for agriculture could come.

Unlike the peasant, for whom every rock, every tree, every particle of earth on his little plot had meaning, the gentry were capable of intellectual detachment. They carried on experiments in crop rotation and stock breeding, and they became promoters of a more scientific agriculture. At the same time, one long step removed from the dirt and fatigue of labor in the fields, they were also capable of a romantic approach to husbandry. Their education in the classics provided them with a wealth of material, and their anxieties about the beginnings of industrial development gave them solid reasons for the formulation of a romantic agrarian myth.

In America, with its abundance of unoccupied land, the myth had many propagators, but none was more fluent in expressing its main themes than Thomas Jefferson. His interest in farming was considerable, and he was a leader in agricultural experimentation. Yet Jefferson's ideas about the place of the farmer in society are perhaps more significant than his own role as a planter. Agriculture was to him primarily not a source of wealth but a way of life which encouraged those virtues upon which popular self-government must rest. In Europe, he wrote in his *Notes on Virginia,* manufacturing was being promoted to support the surplus population that could not gain access to the land. The immensity of the American continent, however, made manufacturing unnecessary here. Our citizens need never occupy workbenches or twirl distaffs. Industry and trade were dependent on customers, and "dependence begets subservience and venality, suffocates the germ of virtue, and prepares fit tools for the designs of ambition." Our workshops therefore could and should remain in Europe.

Bryan refused to say that trade and industry had no place in the American economy, but his emphasis on the primacy of agriculture was Jeffersonian. In accepting the agrarian myth was he not accepting an abstraction, an artificial congeries of images, that could lead men astray? Jerome S. Bruner uses a striking analogy to suggest the relationship between myth and reality. "We know now a new origin of the faint hissing of the sea in a conch shell held to the ear," he writes. "It is in part the tremor and throb of the hand, resonating in the shell's chambers. Yet inescapably, it is the distant sea." Myth making results from man's efforts to make his experience intelligible to himself. Like the roar of the sea in a conch shell, myths grow out of "an external reality and the resonance of the inner vicissitudes of man." Myths are means of ordering the ordinary facts of life. They are never completely false because without the reality they would never exist.

The agrarian myth did have some basis in historical fact. The central figure of the myth was the independent, self-sufficient yeoman. The American environment encouraged—indeed, frequently imposed—self-sufficiency during the early years of settlement. Those who lived in almost complete isolation in the wilderness had no choice but to improvise with the materials they found at hand. Without adequate transportation there was little point in raising crops for market. Until well into the Jackson period, then, there were small, self-sufficient farmers in the United States.

Yet the American environment also helped to bring about the disappearance of the simple yeoman. The very abundance of land and the movement of population westward were factors which encouraged speculation. Unavoidably, commercial attitudes began to appear. Alexis de Tocqueville commented on American agriculture in the 1830's with his usual insight:

> Almost all the farmers of the United States combine some trade with agriculture; most of them make agriculture itself a trade. It seldom happens that an American farmer settles for good upon

the land which he occupies; especially in the districts of the Far West, he brings land into tillage in order to sell it again, and not to farm it; he builds a farmhouse on the speculation that, as the state of the country will soon be changed by the increase of population, a good price may be obtained for it.

While Americans had a tendency to carry "businesslike qualities" and "trading passions" into agriculture, there were other forces at work. The period after 1815 was the seedtime for industry in the United States. Industrial growth during the nineteenth century all but eliminated the way of life portrayed in the agrarian myth, although the myth itself showed remarkable vitality. Believing in it, Bryan used it as a point of departure for his criticism of the way in which American society was developing. He did not stand opposed to industrial advance as such. He conceded that a progressive society should welcome industrial innovation, yet he insisted on the necessity of preserving democratic principles as economic conditions changed. And he doubted that those responsible for industrial expansion had a very high regard for principles.

William McKinley thought differently. He quarreled not with the abstract idea of democracy but with Bryan's agrarian conception of it. As committed to the myth of the self-made man as Bryan was to the agrarian myth, McKinley did not question the new morality that came with industrial expansion. To the captains of industry and their allies the notion that the farmer had a monopoly on virtue was utter nonsense. They built their morality around Darwinian concepts; and Social Darwinism, as the new system of values came to be called, seemed plausible to those who had faith in the myth of the self-made man.

The struggle in the market, so the social Darwinist argument ran, paralleled the struggle for survival in nature. Competition was in both areas hard on individuals; it led to the extinction of some forms of life and ways of life. But if there were individual losers in the struggle, there were general gains. Nature worked always toward higher forms of life. Those organisms that failed to meet the tests of the competition for survival passed out of existence. As in nature, only the best and fittest survived in society so long as government did not interfere to preserve the weaklings. Bryan believed that appropriate legislation would insure the continuation of justice in an age of industrial change. McKinley agreed with most industrialists and financiers that Bryan's legislation was ill-conceived and would lead to injustice.

The expansion of industry thus brought about the conditions out of which the issues of 1896 developed. Industrialization shaped instruments of economic control unknown in Jefferson's day and much more powerful than those he feared. It fixed the locus of political power. Its impact was felt by all Americans as it forced society to face new problems and led some observers to question the adequacy of old institutions. What industrialism meant in terms of production, transportation, organization, and urbanization must therefore be considered in some detail.

The full meaning of industrial development cannot, of course, be read in production statistics, but they do provide some idea of the scope of industrialization and the speed with which it took place. The rate of growth was fastest during the years prior to the Civil War, when fundamental changes in the techniques of production were made and when the factory system replaced household manufactures. During the fifty-year period from 1810 to 1859, the output of American industry increased ten times in value, rising from about $200 million to almost $2 billion. After the Civil War, maturation made the rate of growth slower. Absolute growth was considerably larger, however, for in 1899 the value of manufactured products was $13 billion. Compared with other countries such expansion was striking. In 1860 the United States stood behind the United Kingdom, France, and Germany in the value of manufactures. By 1894 each of those rivals had been outdistanced; indeed, the value of American manufactures was very nearly equal the value of manufactures in all three combined.

The sectional breakdown of industrial production was just as important as the figures on manufacturing in the nation as a whole, and it was to have a definite bearing on the election of 1896. In the period before the Civil War it is clear that the manufacturing center of the country was in the Northeast. In 1860 the value of goods manufactured in the New England and Middle Atlantic States was more than twice as much as the value of goods manufactured in all other states and territories.

The Civil War itself did not bring about rapid industrialization of the Northeast, for that process was already well under way. On the other hand the victory of the North marked the triumph of a predominantly industrial section over a predominantly agricultural section, and it assured the continuing importance of manufacturing in the nation's economy.

In the years after 1865 the basic geographic pattern of manufacturing changed but little in spite of the movement of some industries into the Middle West. At the end of the century industry was still centered in the Northeast. More than half of the goods manufactured in the United States came from New England and the Middle Atlantic States. Three-fourths of American industry was concentrated in the manufacturing belt east of the Mississippi River and north of the Ohio River and the Mason-Dixon line. It was in this region, which in area constituted only one-seventh of the nation, that 75 per cent of the manufacturing wage earners lived. And it was in this region that both Republicans and Democrats campaigned most vigorously in 1896.

By far the most dramatic enterprise in the latter half of the nineteenth century—one certainly not confined to the Northeast—was the development of railroad transportation. At the close of the Civil War there were 35,000 miles of track in operation in the United States. Then came the great era of railroad expansion. By 1873 mileage had doubled. By 1893, when the nation stood poised on the verge of depression, 150,000 new miles had been laid since the Civil War. Small wonder that the major demand for iron in those years came from the railroads.

Statistics on the expansion of the railroad network, like production statistics for manufacturing, are not always complete and are sometimes misleading. The cold figures, furthermore, do not fully explain the social and economic significance of the developments they document. There are, however, certain obvious implications for the farmer in the expansion of the railroad network. Without the means of getting goods to markets, farmers would have had to remain self-sufficient and manufacturers would have had limited markets for their goods. The railroads were, to be sure, not the only means of transportation that might have been used. Parts of the South and West did very nicely with rivers before the railroads were developed. Yet the fact is that railroads became increasingly important as carriers in the latter part of the nineteenth century. For farmers out on the plains they were, indeed, the sole means of transportation.

Clearly technology, industry, and transportation—taken together or separately—mean economic power. The way in which that economic power was exercised and fought for helps to account for the business instability of the age of enterprise. After the Civil War a new kind of speculation based on investments in plant and equipment became increasingly important. And as a national, interdependent economy developed, local and regional fluctuations were felt more keenly.

Railroad promotion and the marketing of railroad securities reflected changes taking place in the American economy. Vigorous, sometimes violent, and often corrupt, railroad men were the first to operate on a grand scale. Jay Gould was perhaps the prototype of men for whom the railroads existed not to provide transportation but to provide speculative opportunities. The willingness of both the national and state governments to subsidize railroads through land grants, loans, mail contracts, and the like made railroad speculation even more attractive. Of course not all railroad promoters were pirates like Gould. But the emphasis on promotional profits led to the construction of lines far in advance of any real need.

Railroads outran the markets for their services, and the results were unhappy for the railroads themselves and for the nation as well. Jay Cooke overextended himself in completing the Northern Pacific, and the failure of his house precipitated the Panic of 1873. Nevertheless in the 1880's another boom in railroad building occurred. The record 12,900 miles constructed in 1887 was one of the causes of the depression of the 1890's. In that decade 30 per cent of all railroad securities then outstanding were subject to receivership proceedings. In the period from 1884 to 1900 some 60,000 miles of railroad were involved in reorganization made necessary through speculative failures.

The overexpansion of railroads which contributed to business instability after the Civil War was at least in part the result of competitive building as railroad men sought greater profits through the elimination of rivals. Similar tendencies can be observed in manufacturing. Technological developments made possible larger industrial plants and factories. The output of manufactured goods after the Civil War increased much more rapidly than the number of factories producing those goods. The desire to make the most of technological efficiency and the increased profits it promised led to an intensification of competition. New large-scale plants drove smaller, less-efficient rivals from business. Sometimes expansion of facilities created surpluses and resulted in competitive price cutting. Improved transportation facilities also contributed to increased competition; firms were provided with the means to market products on a national scale. Gone were the days when a large number of small manufacturers sold their goods in a local market protected from the outside by high transportation costs. The new industrial order was one in which a smaller number of larger firms struggled for control of larger markets.

To the men responsible for directing the destinies of such firms, competition did not seem the life of trade. On the contrary, price competition was potentially ruinous to all. Thus the competing firms in many industries sought to avoid the evils of price rivalry by forming combinations and mergers. The merger movement aroused a profound fear of monopoly. The dangers which were supposed to be inherent in the concentration of economic power account for the passage of the Sherman Anti-Trust Act in 1890. Despite antimonopoly efforts, however, the merger movement continued, and the election of 1896 occurred at a time when it began to pick up speed and momentum. The trend toward consolidation which had been observed by the discerning in the 1870's and 1880's had been but a beginning.

Arising first out of a desire to limit cutthroat competition, mergers brought additional advantages to those who had some part in their development. Bigness seemed to generate its own peculiar rewards. The owners and managers of large combinations gained greater control over supply and demand. They found that new economies could be effected in the procurement of machines and raw materials. Their ability to secure favorable transportation rates and credit terms was enhanced. It was possible to deal more summarily with labor and to organize production more efficiently. Seasonal and other fluctuations could be better planned for and their bad effects minimized. In short it seemed that the economic power which technology, industry, and transportation had created could be most efficiently used when concentrated in the hands of a few. Efforts to prevent the growth of big business were generally as effective as fabled efforts to sweep back the sea.

Coordinate with the development of industry and the concentration of economic power was the growth of cities. Nothing so graphically illustrates the changes taking place in American life in the nineteenth century as the census figures which document that growth. In 1800, the year Jefferson was elected President, only 6 per cent of the population lived in places with 2,500 or more inhabitants. In the entire country there were but six cities with 10,000 or more people. By 1860 the percentage of urban population had increased to almost 20 per cent. It is true that the census did not record more city dwellers than people in rural areas until 1920, but the trend was already apparent when South Carolina cannon opened up on Fort Sumter. In the decade of the 1890's urban population increased from 22 million to 30 million while rural population increased from 41 million to 46 million. The number of cities with 10,000 or more people increased from 354 to 440. When Bryan was telling his fellow Democrats that destruction of agriculture would cause grass to grow in the streets of every city of the country, some 38 per cent of the American people lived in cities.

One or two further items of special interest can be gleaned from census data. In 1860 almost 56 per cent of the nation's population lived in the region extending from New England westward to the Mississippi and southward through Pennsylvania and to the Ohio River. In 1900, despite urban growth throughout the country and despite the fact that population west of the Mississippi had increased rapidly in the period since 1860, the Northeastern and East North Central States still contained almost 49 per cent of the American people. This was the area of crucial importance during the election of 1896.

It should be evident that understanding of the forces which were at work in the late nineteenth century—and specifically those which operated in the election of 1896—requires some understanding of the city and its ways. Developments in industry, technology, and transportation not only made urban growth possible; they made urban growth inevitable. The city was the natural habitat of modern industry in the United States as in Europe. Those who gained control over industry therefore exercised a powerful influence in the economy of the city. The city, unlike the country, however, was made up of men and women with many occupations and widely varied economic interests. The mind of the city was not one mind, but many. It was cosmopolitan in the sense that it was composed of elements gathered from all over the world. This multiplicity and hetereogeneity worked against the emergence of an *idée fixe*. The pluralistic society of the city promoted a pluralistic mentality.

While the captain of industry might be the dominant force in the economy which gave rise to the city, it does not follow therefore that he was the dominant force in the city itself. John D. Rockefeller did much to shape Cleveland's destiny by locating refineries there. Yet his orientation was toward the oil industry, not toward Cleveland. Similarly, Andrew Carnegie located steel plants in the

Pittsburgh district because it was ideally suited to steel production. Although he was more interested in civic matters than most industrial magnates, he was chiefly concerned with his business. There was his treasure and there his heart. Without Rockefeller and Carnegie, Cleveland and Pittsburgh would not have become what they did. Yet such men—despite their philanthropic efforts—were not important primarily for their civic-mindedness.

In the very nature of things they did have a certain indirect influence on attitudes toward the city, an influence which extended far beyond their economic interests. The achievements of captains of industry seemed to imply that the urban scene offered the greatest opportunities. Urban areas became particularly attractive to those who sought to emulate the Carnegies and the Rockefellers. The city, to be sure, had its peculiar sins, traps, and pitfalls, but it was where one had to go if one wished to mount the ladder of success. Those who left the farms to find their fortune in the metropolis did not often succeed in entering the ranks of the captains of industry. Various studies have shown how great were the odds against poor boys who tried to make good. Be that as it may, the motivation that brought them to the city was not likely to blossom into selfless devotion to the welfare of the community. They came asking not what they could do for the city, but what the city could do for them.

Then there were those who lived in urban communities not by choice but by chance. Many were born there, of course, and knowing no other environment were complacent in their acceptance of what the metropolis had to offer. For some, inadequate sewage systems and unpaved streets were so much a part of their existence that they were indifferent to proposed improvements. Others would have liked to escape to the country but were prevented by economic conditions from doing so. The vaunted safety valve which would allow urban workers to escape their environment when conditions became difficult simply did not exist. For every urban laborer who somehow managed to make the move to the country in the late nineteenth century, there were twenty farmers who crowded into the city to compete for jobs.

Slum areas contained a particularly high proportion of persons who might have preferred a rural environment and whose freedom of choice was limited by the need to live—somehow—from day to day. Many of those persons were immigrants who were easily exploited by employers and by city political machines. Bosses and ward heelers often seemed to be the only ones interested in the welfare of the slum dweller. Machine politicians did provide some help. They could usually manage to find at least temporary jobs for the unemployed, and failing that they were ready to tide a man over with a small loan. But of course their motives were far from being altruistic. Their objective was control over city government with its endless possibilities for graft, and the easiest way to gain control was to buy votes with acts of kindness. However inadequate as a system of relief, the methods of the municipal machine were generally successful. Endowed with precious little civic conscience, they were able for years to thwart efforts to establish good government.

Reformers were nothing if not persistent. Settlement houses were established, organizations for municipal improvement were formed, and the squalid conditions which prevailed in the slums were described by writers such as Jacob Riis. Yet the obstacles were considerable, and the heroic labors of humanitarians availed little. A sample of 2,562 families of city wage and clerical workers shows that between 1888 and 1891 the median annual income was something like $380. Even allowing for differences in purchasing power, the figure is appallingly low. It does, however, suggest what may well have been the heart of the urban problem. The cheap labor available in the cities aided manufacturers in their drive to gain economic sovereignty, but the workers themselves could exert virtually no economic influence. Until such time as they could gain what John Kenneth Galbraith calls countervailing power, they would suffer want and the cause of municipal reform would suffer defeat.

This is an important point and it should be emphasized. Urban workers were highly vulnerable to the economic power wielded by employers. They could not easily move, and work was essential if they were to exist even marginally. They therefore faced a situation in which there were many sellers of labor and few buyers. Low wages were the result. Such wages were also a measure of the power of manufacturers who owned the plants in which workers were employed. It is now possible to see why the best efforts of urban reformers were for a long time not enough. Industrialists, who were not primarily interested in the improvement of cities where their factories were located, obeyed impulses which were perfectly natural for men whose major concern was the control of markets for their products. Keeping labor costs at a minimum would help to give them market power. Such a policy would also keep workers in a state where subsistence, not municipal reform, was a dominant objective. In this state they could easily be exploited by the machines which were the opponents of reform. The acquisition of power by labor unions—as much as the cutting off of immigration—was ultimately to change urban environment.

Much of American history in the nineteenth century can be written in terms of the encroachment of the city on rural areas. The railroad network which spread outward from urban centers of industry traced the extent of that encroachment. Some of the most rapidly expanding metropolitan areas in the country—Chicago, Minneapolis-St. Paul, Omaha, Kansas City, St. Louis—could attribute a large share of their growth to the expansion of railroad lines. Of course industrial development soon followed, and in some cases preceded, the railroads. Meat packers set up their plants in Chicago, St. Louis, and Kansas City. Flour milling centered first in Minneapolis and later spread to other cities. Manufacturers of farm machinery found convenient locations in cities close to the fertile prairies of Middle America. Much of the early industry of western cities was related to agriculture. But from simple beginnings the variety of manufactured goods produced in western cities increased as did the population of those cities.

In yet another sense the city encroached on the farmlands. The technology that made industrialization possible was by no means confined to manufacturing. As factories grew first in number and then in size, farming became increasingly mechanized. The use of machinery in agriculture made the rural population more subject to urban influences and more aware of the city. Increased productivity which came with the use of machinery meant that fewer farmers could feed more city dwellers. Farm mechanization therefore contributed to the relative decline of the agricultural population. It also led to an exaggeration of certain trends in American agriculture making farmers more and more dependent on decisions and policies which emanated from the cities and over which they had no control.

The mechanization of agriculture in the United States was not, of course, a sudden phenomenon nor one that was confined to the post-Civil War period. It perhaps had its origins in the emphasis on scientific farming which was so much in vogue in the eighteenth century. Nevertheless the American environment provided a peculiar inducement for the use of machines in farming. Here, on the frontier at least, there was an abundance of land but a scarcity of labor. This led to an early emphasis on extensive rather than intensive farming and encouraged inventions which would increase the farmer's efficiency.

On the eve of the Civil War farm implements and machinery in use throughout the nation were valued at $246 million. By the turn of the century the value had increased to some $761 million. This increase might seem surprisingly low in view of the fact that in the same period the number of farms increased from 2,044,000 to 5,737,000 and the land in farms from 407,179,000 acres to 838,583,000 acres. Thus the average value of implements per farm increased only from $120 to $133. But mechanization was vastly more significant than these figures suggest. For one thing, machinery became more efficient and proportionately cheaper with the passage of time. Furthermore there were great differences in the extent to which different sections of the country became mechanized. The value of southern farm machinery in 1900 was not even half of what it had been in 1860. The value of farm machinery in the rest of the country almost doubled between 1860 and 1900. And almost half of the 1900 valuation was in the twelve North Central States.

The increased use of machinery had little effect on productivity per acre. The average yield varied according to climatic conditions but not according to mechanization. Agricultural implements were significant because they increased production per man-hour and decreased costs per unit of production. Estimates on man-hour productivity vary, and it is doubtless wise not to rely too heavily on them. According to one of these, 3.73 man-hours of labor were required to produce one bushel of wheat in 1800, while in 1900 one bushel of wheat required 1.08 man-hours. Fred Shannon, taking a somewhat different approach, came up with rather more satisfactory figures. He estimated that working one acre of wheat by hand methods required 61 hours, 5 minutes; by machine methods the same acre required 3 hours, 19.2 minutes. The labor cost was reduced from $3.55 to 66 cents. Similar economies in time and labor costs could be effected in other crops. The important fact is that the standard of progress in the United States was not productivity per acre, as in countries where intensive agriculture was practiced, but productivity per man-hour.

The kind of progress that came with developing agricultural technology, then, enabled the farmer to cultivate increasing amounts of land or work the same land more efficiently. To buy the machines necessary for successful competition with other producers, however, he often had to go into debt. He had to take risks, but the whole history of American agriculture encouraged such gambling on the future. As has been pointed out, farmers had long been accustomed to speculation in land, depending on an increase in land values for at least part of their livelihood. But if land speculation had rather consistently worked to their advantage, mechanization brought with it some unsuspected hazards. For one thing it led to the cultivation of semiarid areas of the Great Plains that probably should have remained grassland. Once those regions were subjected to the plow, the number of crops that could be grown successfully was more limited than in regions where rainfall was greater. Cash crop cultivation was especially prevalent there, as it was in the South. The difficulty with placing so much emphasis on a single crop, of course, was that farmers increased their risks. Entering more completely into the cash-market economy, they were more likely to be seriously hurt by falling prices, more inclined to fail during years of drouth, and more dependent on the railroads and other distributive facilities.

Farmers with capital adequate to weather periods of crisis, along with those who practiced diversified farming, were able to succeed. Unfortunately, however, too many men in the trans-Mississippi West were overly optimistic. Counting far too strongly on continuing bumper crops, and failing to see that cultivation of hitherto untapped lands might bring about overproduction and falling prices, they mortgaged themselves more extensively than was justifiable. Farmers in the South, for somewhat different reasons, also suffered from too much specialization and not enough capital. Sharecropping and the crop-lien system—in themselves suggestive of insufficient capital—led to heavy overemphasis on cotton and made any attempt to limit its production impossible.

The long and the short of it was that farmers had become businessmen, but the commercialization of agriculture left many of them in a very poor competitive position. On the plains and in the South they did not have the market power of the industrialist, the implements manufacturer, and others who sold to them. Nor did they have the market power of the grain dealers and other processors who bought from them. Farmers at noncompetitive points could not bargain effectively with railroads.

In the summer of 1890, the Omaha *World Herald* posed the question: "What ails the farmer?" In the first place, commented the paper in answering its own question, farmers were in debt and heavily mortgaged. The farmer was not troubled so much by lack of productivity; through hard work he raised abundant crops. The trouble began when he tried to turn his crops into money. "With a rate of interest amounting to as much as the rental of a farm, exorbitant transportation charges to a market, where he is put into competition with pauper labor and cheap American made machinery, and with double prices charged him for everything that he and his family eats or uses or wears, the answer to the question 'What ails the farmer?' is not far to seek."

In 1891 the *World Herald* noted that the cost of shipping 400 bushels of corn from Bancroft, Nebraska, to Omaha was $42, while the cost for an equivalent distance in Iowa was $13. In Lyons, Nebraska, one man paid $38.50 for freight on a carload of lumber from Omaha; in Iowa the rate would have been $12. Iowa, though it enjoyed some advantages, was not always regarded as a paradise. "I want to tell you Mr. Dolliver," wrote a hardware dealer to his senator in 1896, "that I have lived in Iowa now nearly forty years. I can remember back as far as 1858, and I have never seen such hard times as these are."

Both William Jennings Bryan and William McKinley sought a mixed economy in which interrelated parts might work harmoniously. Yet in the decade of the nineties the multiple relationships between industry and agriculture, management and labor, farm and city were far from benign. Workers charged that they were being exploited by expanding industry and began to agitate for a redress of grievances. The growing power of captains of industry and finance posed a serious threat to agriculture, or so the farmers thought. Signs of unrest multiplied as depression followed the Panic of 1893. Economic harmony began to seem less a real possibility than a desperate hope.

Neither Bryan nor McKinley grew despondent; neither permitted himself to become disillusioned. Far more than McKinley, however, Bryan urged the necessity of action. Identifying with the yeoman of the agrarian myth, he was naturally critical of industrialization, and he viewed captains of industry as leading the hosts of wickedness. Although he knew he could not restore the Jeffersonian world, he yearned for the ethical purity which he associated with that world. And he was prepared to act in the interest of economic justice as agrarians conceived it.

McKinley, on the other hand, instinctively favored business and the self-made men who presumably dominated it. He did not dislike farmers or industrial workers, nor did he ever immodestly assert his own superiority to other men. But he could not see how justice would result from government intervention in behalf of misfits who had failed to survive the competion of the market. He could still affirm the inevitability of economic harmony if such men would give up their agitation, accept a lesser role in society, and allow successful businessmen and industrialists to work for the common good while pursuing their own enlightened self-interest.

The two myths which dominated American thought in the nineteenth century were real enough in themselves precisely because they did dominate American thought. Bryan's acceptance of the agrarian myth and McKinley's belief in the myth of the self-made man help to explain why neither candidate offered a completely new departure, a radical alternative, in 1896. Each spoke in an idiom to which Americans had grown accustomed. Each held a position ultimately justified by a traditional myth.

Even though the myths were made credible by American experience, they had deficiencies when used to interpret economic realities. The myth of the self-made man, especially when expressed in the scientific terminology of Social Darwinism, seemed to account for the success of the captains of industry. During the depression of the 1890's, however, people began to ask what had gone wrong. They began to ask for explanations not of success but of failure. McKinley responded plausibly enough, yet he said nothing to break down long-held economic prejudices. Not until after he became President would he fully explore new lines of thought on economic questions.

Bryan doubtless felt himself better equipped than McKinley to offer solutions to the problems of the nineties. He spoke for the weak and the downtrodden, for the common man whose lot was never as good as it might have been and who felt most keenly the impact of depression. Yet Bryan's identification with the long-suffering yeoman worked against a thorough apprehension of the predicament in which urban laborers found themselves. He sympathized with industrial workers, and he developed his arguments with them in mind, but he never really penetrated to a deep understanding of their needs.

Both McKinley and Bryan were men of good will. Both sought to do what was right. Both were expert political practitioners. Yet neither was prepared to look squarely at the realities of American economic development; neither could resist ordering facts to fit a mythological frame of reference. The true realists of 1896 were those who sought to rid themselves of preconceptions, who tried to examine the realities themselves, and who formulated programs without resort to traditional images. There were a few such men, yet a great majority of Americans did not think to ask if there was any merit in their approach. Ironically, it was such realists and their followers who were most vigorously branded as impractical visionaries.

III

FARMERS ORGANIZE

❁

POLITICAL REALISM INVOLVES MORE THAN CLEVER campaigning and shrewd analysis of voting patterns. In fact, hard-headed practical politics of the kind that wins elections is not necessarily realistic. Politicians who have prided themselves on being practical have characteristically conducted campaigns with both hope and fear—hope of attracting votes and fear of giving offense. They have been more responsive to voter opinion than to the needs of society. In contrast to such political practicalism, realism may require a thorough-going reappraisal of society and society's needs. William McKinley, whose stock in trade consisted of traditional images and forms, was more practical than he was realistic. Although Bryan demonstrated a willingness to follow a more unorthodox course, he too had his practical side. With his Jeffersonian faith in the wisdom of the people, he was always reluctant to push them further than they seemed willing to go.

More realistic (in the sense that they were ready to take a fresh look at economic realities) than either McKinley or Bryan were some of the radical reformers who became associated with the Populist movement of the nineties. Developing out of acute agricultural unrest, Populism assumed the truth of the agrarian myth. Yet it did not remain merely a farmers' movement. The People's party eventually seemed to provide the organizational structure for cooperation between farmers and urban workers. Among those who hoped to bring about a farmer-labor coalition under Populist auspices were leaders imaginative enough to throw aside traditional conceptions. Their plans for a new organization which would break the cake of political custom were the outcome of their realistic analysis of economic conditions. Efforts to unite farmers and workers came closest to reaching fruition in the later stages of the Populist movement, however, and detailed discussion of those efforts must be deferred. This chapter is concerned with the emergence of farm organizations and with the formation of the People's party.

In its beginnings the Populist movement was similar to the Granger movement of the 1870's. Indeed, the People's party has sometimes been regarded as the successor of the Patrons of Husbandry. Both organizations were devoted to the welfare of farmers, and both looked toward the advancement of agricultural interests. There was nevertheless an important difference between the two. Although its members were active in politics, particularly in securing railroad rate legislation, the Grange never became a political party like the People's party. It sought to place men and principles first, and as an organization it concentrated on business and educational enterprises. Unfortunately for the Patrons of Husbandry, its ventures in cooperative business activity were overly ambitious, and several failures helped to bring about its decline.

When the Granger movement came to a standstill, other organizations appeared in agricultural regions of the West and South. Of more or less simultaneous origin, the new farmers' clubs arose out of local needs. The contemporaries of Bryan and McKinley found their most meaningful social and political relationships in the neighborhood. It was natural that with the decline of the Patrons of Husbandry, a national organization, they should look to local associations to further their objectives. Of course the various societies soon began to coalesce into a farmers' movement of national scope. Yet from first to last, the particularistic interests of agrarians were much in evidence, sometimes working against a truly effective national organization.

Among the most important of the early farmers' clubs was one begun in Lampasas County, Texas, in 1874 or 1875. Its purpose was to encourage cooperation in catching horse thieves, in opposing the activities of land speculators and cattle barons, and in purchasing supplies. After struggling along on the ragged edge of survival for several years, the Texas organization obtained a charter in 1880 as the Farmers' State Alliance. The decade of the eighties saw more rapid growth; by 1885 the Alliance boasted 50,000 members. Soon steps were being taken toward union with other farm groups. It was Dr. C. W. Macune who took the lead in negotiations that resulted in a merger with the 10,000 member Louisiana Farmers' Union in 1887. Macune was elected president of the new order, the National Farmers' Alliance and Cooperative Union of America; and with missionary ardor he preached a program of expansion.

In the meantime, another organization of farmers in Arkansas, the Agricultural Wheel, was growing at an equally impressive rate. Begun in the early eighties as a debating society, the Wheel had achieved status as a state organization in 1883. Two years later, after it had absorbed the Brothers of Freedom, it could claim a membership of 40,000. This increased more than tenfold in the next two years. Could a union of the Wheel and the Alliance be effected? There were obstacles in the way: each had its own ritual, its own character, and its own pretensions. But after several conferences a consolidation of forces was completed in the fall of 1889. The new organization was christened first the National Farmers' and Laborers' Union, and then later the name was changed to the National Farmers' Alliance and Industrial Union. The N.F.A. and I.U., or simply the Southern Alliance as it came to be called, was destined to become the largest farm organization in the United States in the early nineties. It spread into every southern state and several northern ones, ultimately registering a membership of nearly three million.

If the Southern Alliance invaded the North, however, it was not because northern farmers lacked organizations. During the years in which the Alliance was taking shape through a process of amalgamation in the South, a similar body was being formed in the Northwest. What C. W. Macune was to southern farmers, Milton George was to northern farmers. Editor of a Chicago farm journal, the *Western Rural,* George conceived of an alliance for his section in 1880. Familiarizing himself with various experiments in farmers' unions, he publicized the alliance idea in the columns of his newspaper. Like the Southern Alliance, George's association (the National Farmers' Alliance) went through a time of troubles in the early eighties. With good crops and fair prices, farmers were not inclined to join any groups. But with a drop in prices in the fall and winter of 1884-1885 came a revival of interest in organization. Farmers on the Plains, especially, got the Alliance religion.

As membership in the Northern Alliance approached the two-million mark, there was considerable talk of another merger, one which would unite the farmers of the nation into one gigantic order. The two alliances had many things in common. They were one in their agrarianism, in their acceptance of the myth of rural virtue, in their consciousness of an encroaching industrialism, in their fear of monopoly. Yet differences between them were, if they were not fundamental, at least significant. For one thing, the Southern Alliance was a secret order and restricted its membership to white farmers. The Northern Alliance, on the other hand, shunned secrecy and extended membership to anyone who had been born on a farm whether he continued to live there or not.

The whole question of Negro participation was one which caused no end of trouble for the Southern Alliance, and it insinuated itself into every discussion of merger. Most southerners would recognize the existence of a Colored Farmers' Alliance—indeed, could see some advantage in having a parallel organization—but that was as far as they were willing to go. They were extremely reluctant to take any steps which might jeopardize white supremacy in the South. This is why the Southern Alliancemen, unlike their northern brethren, hesitated to join any third-party movement. They preferred to concentrate on economic activities and to work through the Democratic party toward whatever political objectives they thought necessary. In that manner they could avoid splitting the white vote.

Among the schemes which many members of the Southern Alliance particularly favored was the subtreasury plan. This plan looked toward the establishment of subtreasuries and warehouses in all rural counties. The subtreasuries would be authorized to accept nonperishable farm products for storage. They would have the power to make loans at 1 per cent interest up to four-fifths of the value of the deposited product. The money so borrowed would have to be returned with interest before products could be removed; the time limit for storage was to be one year. When he left his product at the warehouse, however, the farmer would receive a certificate of deposit, and this certificate would be negotiable. The subtreasury plan was designed to accomplish two ends: it would, thought its supporters, enable farmers to obtain easy credit, and it would enable them to sell their produce if they so desired at opportune times.

Opponents of the plan were quick to point out what they regarded as its shortcomings, and to attack the "hayseed socialists" who sponsored it. *Frank Leslie's Newspaper*, for example, thought it involved nothing less than the establishment of "Governmental pawnshops" on a grand scale. "The Farmers' Alliance," said the Philadelphia *North American*, "does not want money. It wants due bills. It wants pawn tickets; and though its chiefs do not know a mowing machine from a grub, they want the earth." While invective doubtless outweighed argument, even some farmers opposed the subtreasury with what seemed good reason. Although no one questioned the feasibility of storing cotton, many would classify western grains as perishable and therefore unfit for storage. Thus the subtreasury plan became another point at issue between the Northern and the Southern Alliance.

The divisions within the alliance movement were not only geographical. Perhaps the most basic disagreement was over the very nature of the Alliance itself, and here debate centered on a question that cut across sectional lines: should a farmers' organization seek to gain its objectives through political action, or should it compete directly in the market place? From the beginning interest in politics and in political action ran high. Yet for various reasons leaders in both North and South insisted that the alliance movement remain nonpartisan; ostensibly at least, they would not affiliate with any party, nor would they seek to form a party of their own. The southerner's reluctance to break with the Democracy aside, recruitment of new members in all sections of the country was made easier by keeping the organization nonpartisan. During the early years, therefore, the most important Alliance activities were economic ones.

Alliancemen in their search for a means of gaining market power experimented with a variety of plans. On a local level farmers sometimes established cooperative stores or contracted with a merchant to provide goods at a fixed percentage of the cost in return for Alliance patronage. Other experiments were considerably more ambitious and correspondingly more risky. There were stock company schemes whereby central agencies supplied local groups. In some states exchanges were set up for cooperative buying and selling. In others farmers developed plans under which state purchasing agents were appointed to make what bargains they could.

Few of the alliance cooperatives enjoyed success, but the most spectacular failure was that of the Texas Exchange which opened its doors in the fall of 1887 only to close them permanently less than two years later. In large part a product of Macune's fertile brain and soaring ambition, the project called for the sale of agricultural produce and the purchase of farmers' supplies through central headquarters in Dallas. Necessary capital was to be raised by an assessment of two dollars for each member of the state Alliance, and control of the Exchange was vested in an elected board of trustees. The city of Dallas, caught up in the spirit of enterprise which permeated the Alliance, provided a temporary location, a $10,000 subsidy, and promise of a building site. At first the Exchange concerned itself primarily with marketing cotton and grain and with purchasing farm implements at discount prices. Gradually it expanded into dry goods and groceries, in some respects anticipating the shopping center of the future. There was one catch however; farmers did not have the cash to buy. To break the crop-lien system, the Exchange would have to extend credit. The credit plan proved disastrous, for banks refused to honor executed notes upon which the Exchange had contracted to deliver goods. Somehow the inevitable collapse was avoided for a few months, but then it came with a crash. A shadow fell over Macune's reputation, and Alliancemen were led to question the feasibility of such schemes.

Yet the real difficulty lay less in the idea than in its execution. Not that the Texas Exchange was unique in this respect; most cooperatives had similar problems. Lacking the capital which the size of their operations required, they borrowed too heavily at high interest rates. Lacking experienced managers, they sold too cheaply. Lacking esteem in the business community, they were also hampered by the indifference of farmers. The Texas Exchange raised only about $85,000 from assessments and other resources at a time when sound business principles demanded $500,000. Goods were sold at a mere 10 per cent above cost, which of course did not allow enough to meet expenses. Macune proved to be much less skillful in business administration than he was persuasive in oratory. And so it went—the Alliance seemed to be following the Granger pattern. Small wonder that Alliancemen became more receptive to the suggestions of those who were urging political action.

Actually the ground for political action had already been prepared at an important gathering which took place in December, 1889. By mutual agreement the two Alliances, North and South, held annual meetings in St. Louis that year. The idea was that plans for a union could then be worked out. Also on the scene were representatives of the Colored Alliance and the Knights of Labor. Nothing came of the merger talks. The Southern Alliance with some 200 delegates to the North's 75 was by far the stronger of the two organizations, not only at St. Louis but throughout the country. It could afford to be magnanimous and it was. It was even willing to strike the word "white" from membership qualifications, leaving the states to pass upon the eligibility of Negroes. But it would not abandon the secrecy which its leaders thought essential to united action. Northerners, for their part, felt uneasy about affiliating with any group in which they themselves were certain to be a minority. So the advocates of amalgamation might well have considered the St. Louis meeting a failure.

Yet the meetings were not a total loss. Both Alliances drew up platforms, a move which in itself pointed toward political action. Although no third party was formed at this time, all observers agreed that the farmers would exert political influence in the future. The only questions remaining were where and how that influence would be exercised. "At present the whole thing is in a nebulous condition," noted the New York *Sun* early in 1890. Then it added with considerable prescience, "If the reports are to be trusted, a big political movement, which is likely to result in some startling political changes, has begun."

As for the platforms adopted at St. Louis, they were essentially summaries of agrarian demands in the three fundamental areas of land, transportation, and finance. With both Alliances seeking to satisfy as many farmers as possible, the two platforms were the same except for slight differences in emphasis. They called for legislation against alien land ownership and the reclamation of land controlled by aliens, foreign syndicates, and railroads. Several planks concerned with finance clearly revealed that both Alliances favored an inflationary currency, although only the platform of the Southern Alliance mentioned free silver. Clauses urging government ownership and control of railroads were inserted in both platforms. Even though most southerners had doubts about any measure which would mean an increase in the power of the central government, they accepted the railroad proposal because it appealed to labor and to northern farmers.

The Southern Alliance made much of the fact that these demands were drawn up in consultation with representatives of the Knights of Labor. Terence V. Powderly, Grand Master of the union, actually had been thinking in such terms for some time. In October, 1888, he had written James B. Weaver that he hoped "to begin an agitation on three distinct lines, finance, transportation and land." He thought that if the issues were kept before the public the political parties would have to recognize them at least by 1892. "Parties have heretofore been allowed to make their own platforms, without consulting the people," he wrote; "let us give them our views, instruct them what to do and oblige them to make platforms to suit the people." But who, really, were the people for whom the Southern Alliance now presumed to speak in 1889? No matter how much might be said about the cooperation of laborers and mechanics, no matter how much in agreement Powderly may have been with the St. Louis platform, it is obvious that the people who really counted in Alliance thinking were the farmers. Interests that were vital to farmers were peripheral to labor, and interests that were vital to labor were ignored by the Alliance.

Nevertheless, the St. Louis discussions did provide a stimulus to election activities in which it was thought that labor might share. The story of Alliance fireworks and personalities in the campaign of 1890 is an oft-told tale. Every schoolboy who has read his textbook knows something about the colorful eccentrics—"Whiskers" Peffer, "Sockless Jerry" Simpson, Ben Tillman, the "one-eyed ploughboy," Ignatius Donnelly, the brilliant and erratic sage of Nininger, Minnesota, and Tom Watson, the defender of underdogs—who emerged that year as leaders of agrarian radicals. Few students get through a basic course in American history without finding out what Mary Elizabeth Lease said to Kansas farmers.

Far more important than eccentricities and oratory, however, were steps taken toward the formation of a new party in the northwestern states and maneuvers within the Democracy of the South. Out in Kansas the task of organizing the state for the achievement of Alliance objectives was entrusted not to the Alliance itself but to a convention which met in Topeka on June 12, 1890. That convention, made up of delegates from the Alliance, the Knights of Labor, the Farmers' Mutual Benefit Association, and the Patrons of Husbandry, set up a new party and called it the People's party. Other middle western states took similar action. A convention of dissident groups, meeting in Lincoln on July 29, formed the Nebraska People's Independent party. The Dakotas, Minnesota, Colorado, Michigan, and Indiana all had people's or independent parties in 1890. Iowa and Illinois would probably have followed suit had they been holding state-wide elections. In the meantime, Alliancemen in the South had been working to take over control of the Democratic party. Throughout the region the spirit of revolt against the ruling Bourbon aristocracy ran high, especially so in the Carolinas and Georgia.

Results of the election increased the confidence of agrarians in both South and West. The Alliance gained control of legislatures in eight southern states. Alliance-backed candidates won gubernatorial races in South Carolina, Georgia, Tennessee, and Texas. Forty-four newly elected congressmen from the South were in sympathy with the St. Louis platform. Independent victories in Kansas and Nebraska were the most impressive in the West. In Kansas the People's party elected five congressmen and one senator and controlled the lower house of the state legislature. In Nebraska, the Republicans retained control of state offices, but the Independents received a majority in the legislature. A Democrat, an Independent, and a fusionist were victorious in the Nebraska congressional races. The third party held the balance of power in South Dakota and Minnesota. In other middle western states Independent candidates ran well enough to inspire great hopes for the future.

With the showing of 1890, Alliancemen began to talk even more excitedly about the prospects for a national third party. This was the chief topic of conversation as the Southern Alliance prepared for its convention at Ocala, Florida, in December. As might have been predicted the proponents of a third party were middle westerners; southerners countered with the argument that there was now a real opportunity to capture the Democratic party nationally. Macune came up with a compromise proposal which was adopted by the convention: to defer action until early in 1892. At that time a body composed of delegates from all interested groups could determine whether or not to form a national third party. Until then the Alliance could concentrate on the development of its program. The Ocala platform reiterated the St. Louis demands. The controversial subtreasury plan, the only major addition, was included despite opposition; to win over northerners the convention suggested that loans be made on real estate as well as on crops.

Third-party advocates were not to be put off by a discussion of the subtreasury or anything else. They did not propose to languish until 1892. Eager to be up and doing in a party of their own, they issued the call for a conference to meet in Cincinnati in May, 1891. There was nothing secret or exclusive about this conclave. On the afternoon of the 19th into the Music Hall they came—the reformers and nonconformists of every shade and description who had been invited. "Besides the pretended representatives of the staid, sober and patriotic farmer," noted the hostile Nashville *American*, "there were gathered there Knights of Labor, Henry Georgeites, Edward Bellamyites, Prohibitionists and all the detached ites and ists of the country, besides a job lot of miscellaneous and unclassified patriots who freely added their noise and fragrance to the perfume and melody of the occasion." Only loyal Alliancemen from the South seemed ill at ease. Leonidas L. Polk, President of the Southern Alliance, declined to attend but sent a letter urging caution. Of the 1,400-odd delegates who were seated, only 36 came from Southern states. That such a convention of the heterodox should be able to reach a consensus was a mark of its political success. It summarized and endorsed the Ocala demands, along with resolutions passed by the Northern Alliance convention in Omaha the previous January. Near unanimity on objectives, however, did not mean complete agreement on how to achieve those objectives.

As it turned out, two factions developed. One, led by Ignatius Donnelly, would gladly have formed a new party on the spot. The other, a more conservative group headed by James B. Weaver, preferred to wait until the presidential year itself. Weaver had had long experience in politics, and his judgment carried weight. He had been a Free Soiler and a Republican in Iowa prior to the Civil War. Returning to his home state after a successful career in the Union army, he had held several minor political positions. His views on railroad regulation and currency had alienated fellow Republicans, however, and he had joined the Greenback party. Elected to Congress on the Greenback ticket in 1878, he had been the party's candidate for President in 1880. He had again won a seat in the House in 1884 and had been re-elected in 1886. He had been active in the Alliance, and he was to become one of the most important leaders of the People's party.

In view of Weaver's cautious counsel, the ingenious Donnelly arranged a "compromise" which was not really a compromise at all. He agreed that the final arrangements for the third party could be made at a convention to be held on Washington's birthday, 1892. But in the meantime, the resolutions prepared by the Donnelly committee called for immediate formation of the People's party and the appointment of a national executive committee. If the convention of February 22 did not carry through on its duties, this committee would be authorized to go ahead and call a national convention to name a candidate for President. The Donnelly faction had won a clear victory (after all, a new party had been formed on the spot!) yet all sides, including the Southern Alliance, could express satisfaction that the principal action would not be taken until 1892.

Regardless of timing, however, success depended on the participation of the Southern Alliance. Without the support of the largest farmers' organization in the country, no third-party effort would get very far. Happily for the third-party men, straws in the wind revealed a weakening of the southern farmer's loyalty to the Democracy. When the Supreme Council of the Southern Alliance met in Indianapolis in November, 1891, members seemed willing to listen to the arguments of the People's party executive committee. Die-hards who would not submit to the third-party force withdrew from the Alliance. Alliancemen who remained voted with enthusiasm to instruct their congressmen not to be bound by the Democratic caucus in the forthcoming choice of a Speaker. Although not all Alliance congressmen went along with this suggestion, Tom Watson and eight others rejected the caucus choice and threw in with third-party forces.

The grand conclave at St. Louis, when it finally met in February, 1892, turned out to be everything that Ignatius Donnelly and other third-party advocates had hoped it might be. Like the Cincinnati conference, this was a reform convention, not merely an alliance affair. Various competing organizations scrambled for seats so vigorously that the credentials committee was hard put to complete its chores within a reasonable time. Among the eight hundred or so delegates finally seated there were twenty-two separate orders represented. The most important contest, one that suggested clearly the temper of the gathering, involved the Georgia Alliance delegation. The convention voted with alacrity to seat the third-party men from Georgia rather than those who opposed independent political action. Another third-party victory came with the selection of Leonidas L. Polk as permanent chairman. While no one could disparage his services to the Alliance, he was nevertheless a recent convert to the third-party idea.

Still, the question of independent political action had to be handled with delicacy and finesse. To ram through an endorsement of the People's party without gentlemanly consideration of southern sensibilities would never do, and those in control of the convention knew it. Instead of dallying with an issue on which there was disagreement, the convention concentrated on the formulation of demands which had been reiterated again and again: a flexible national currency; free and unlimited coinage of silver; a graduated income tax; postal savings banks; reclamation of alien land holdings, and of lands held by railroads in excess of needs. The subtreasury, which was more attractive to the South, was balanced by a demand for government ownership and operation of railroads, which appealed more to the North.

In writing of those proposals, conservative journalists dipped their pens in acid. "If it were possible to carry out this mad scheme of the howlers and cranks the Nation would soon be in a terrible plight," fulminated the Chicago *Tribune*. "It would make so much party patronage as to convert the Administration into a National Tammany Hall and establish in power a centralized corrupt robber despotism that could not be deposed at the ballot-box, but only got rid of by a bloody civil war." The *Tribune* concluded that "the entire scheme of these fellows could only be matched by the inmates of a lunatic asylum for vagary and folly, and by those of a penitentiary for dishonesty and rascality of purpose." Conservative newspapers never seemed able to take the agrarian radical seriously—they were forever poking fun at his dress, his whiskers, and his mannerisms—but they frequently took far too seriously the extreme statements which appeared in their own columns.

In the arts of rhetoric, the city slickers of the press met their match in men such as Ignatius Donnelly, Leonidas Polk, or "Cyclone" Davis of Texas. When the formation of a third party at St. Louis appeared certain, Donnelly predicted a political wedding of the old parties. "The ceremony will be performed at the altar of plutocracy. Grover Cleveland and Ben Harrison will act as brides-maids, the devil will give away the bride, and Jay Gould will pronounce the benediction." Touching on fundamental issues of section and class, Donnelly thundered on: "We propose to wipe the Mason and Dixon line out of our geography; to wipe the color line out of politics; to give Americans prosperity, that the man who creates shall own what he creates; to take the robber class from the throat of industry; to take possession of the government of the United States, and put our nominee in the White House."

Third-party men were as gifted in parliamentary footwork as in oratory. In a neat bit of political manipulation, the convention adjourned after the adoption of the platform. But only a few disgruntled delegates left the hall. According to a previously developed plan, the majority who remained reconstituted themselves as a mass meeting of "citizens who love their country." General Weaver took the chair, and to him went the responsibility of appointing a committee of fifteen to work with the executive committee of the People's party. The date for a nominating convention could now be set, and final arrangements could be made.

The efforts of third-party men came to a climax with the gathering of farmers and reformers in Omaha, site of the People's party convention. Asked to be on hand Saturday, July 2, so that a convention organization could be established in time to make nominations on the 4th, delegates arrived with every incoming train on Friday. By evening street corners and hotel corridors were crowded with people engaged in earnest discussion. Whatever one might call them—hayseeds, unwashed masses, horny-handed sons of toil, plain folks, producers of wealth which they themselves did not enjoy—these delegates were not, for the most part, professional politicians. But what they lacked in sophistication, they made up in seriousness of purpose. In the lobby of the Millard Hotel, where there was standing room only, they held an impromptu mass meeting. Speakers addressed the throng from the grand staircase, and from this point on until it adjourned in the early morning hours the following Tuesday, the convention resembled a camp meeting in its intensity.

Early on Saturday, H. E. Taubeneck, Chairman of the National Committee, called the convention to order at the Coliseum. The preliminaries were dull, and not until the afternoon session did anyone strike fire. Then the Lincoln Glee Club started it with a song which ridiculed the argument that farmers were benefited by a protective tariff:

> 'Tis true, we haven't Sunday Clothes, nor very much to eat,
> And corn is good for nothing now except for making heat;
> We haven't laid a dollar by for all our toil and sweat,
> But still we're very thankful that we have the tariff yet.

The performance brought down the house, and delegates were in a proper mood to listen to Ignatius Donnelly, ablest of the Populist orators. "If liberty fails here it fails forever," he warned. "This is the battle of mankind. It emphasizes the death of sectionalism." Here a black-bearded Pennsylvanian leaped to his feet shouting, "Amen, amen, let the people say amen to that." And the response came in a mighty chorus. Donnelly then proceeded to his conclusion. There must be no talk of failure here in this movement that was the culmination of all the world's battles for right and liberty. The People's party had enlisted in the campaign with every intention of winning, and win it would.

After similar exhortations the convention adjourned until Monday. Delegates did not spend the Sabbath in idleness, however, for several gatherings had been planned. Followers of Edward Bellamy met to discuss nationalist doctrine. The disciples of Henry George listened to Hamlin Garland read "Under the Lion's Paw." Susan B. Anthony held forth at still another meeting of those interested in the cause of women's suffrage. A large number attended memorial services in honor of Leonidas L. Polk, who had died shortly before the convention. A gifted leader and a man who commanded universal respect, Polk had been one of those favored to win the party's presidential nomination.

Two major items of business confronted the delegates when they reassembled on the Fourth: the adoption of a platform and the naming of a ticket. The report of the Resolutions Committee contained no surprises; much of it was a reworking of the platform adopted in St. Louis in February. All present and accounted for were the familiar demands for a more flexible currency, for free coinage of silver, for an increase in the circulating medium, for a graduated income tax, for a subtreasury, for postal savings banks, for government ownership and operation of railroads, and for the reclamation of lands held by aliens and railroads.

"Every sentence of the eloquent paper was greeted with applause," reported the Omaha *World Herald*. When the silver plank was read, the Texas delegation rose to demand three cheers for silver. The three cheers were still echoing from the rafters when the black-bearded Pennsylvanian in the amen corner shouted, "Amen, let everybody say amen to that." Again the chorus responded. But these outbursts were nothing compared to the wild enthusiasm that prevailed when the reading of the platform had been completed. Hats and coats were thrown in the air. Excited men seized state guidons and paraded around the Coliseum. Delegates and spectators joined in a strange, brawling demonstration that almost resembled the ritualistic dance of a primitive people. For thirty-eight minutes the delirium persisted. Finally relative calm was restored. "The old parties go wild over their candidates," Chairman Henry L. Loucks told the convention. "We go wild over our principles. There is a difference."

Principles or no, a candidate still had to be chosen. For some time the nomination of Judge Walter Q. Gresham, later to become Secretary of State under Cleveland, seemed a real possibility. Herman E. Taubeneck and others did their best to bring it about, but the Judge notified the convention that he was not available. James B. Weaver then appeared as the logical choice, and he won on the first ballot. For his running mate the convention selected Virginia's James G. Field. Weaver was doubtless the best candidate the Populists had; he was certainly a seasoned campaigner. Yet he had fought in perhaps too many causes. "He is the sort of man who is always ready to take up with any new organization which can give him either office or prominence," said *The Nation* in the sort of attack that became typical, "and no platform could be constructed so ridiculous that he would not gladly stand upon it. He is the fit product of a convention in which Ignatius Donnelly was one of the most popular orators."

Shortly after his nomination Weaver told a Des Moines audience that the movement for which he spoke could be summed up in a single phrase: "Equal rights for all and special privileges for none." His task, as he conceived it, was to expound the only platform of 1892 based on that premise. Weaver and his wife, in the company of Populist leaders including Mrs. Lease, toured both West and South in a campaign of education. In the far West the group found considerable enthusiasm for free silver, but in the South they encountered difficulties. Resentful of attempts to disrupt the one-party system and with it white supremacy, extremists pelted Weaver with a mixture of threats, epithets, and rotten eggs. They made him, according to Mrs. Lease, "a regular walking omelet." In spite of this, the Populists were optimistic. "If we cannot elect our man," said Senator Kyle of South Dakota, "we can at least throw the election into the House of Representatives."

It did not work out that way. In the election which Cleveland won with a plurality of 501,425 popular votes, Weaver and Field polled 1,026,816. The Democrats received 45.8 per cent of the total, the Republicans 42.6 per cent, and the Populists only 8.4 per cent. For the first time since the Civil War, however, a third party broke into the electoral college where the Weaver and Field ticket received 22 votes. Kansas, North Dakota, and Colorado elected Populist governors. Weaver publicly expressed satisfaction with the results of the election, claiming that the People's party now held the balance of power in a majority of the states. In the West, where fusion with the Democrats had proved rewarding, Populist morale was at its peak. Throughout the country, party members thought the future promising.

Clearly America was passing through a critical period, and her citizens were approaching an hour of decision. The Harrison administration had been turned out of office, and Republicans were looking for a new leader. Jubilant Democrats had elected a President and had won majorities in both houses of Congress, but their elation was to be short-lived. Influences bringing about depression were already at work, and economic pressures were to split the party. Populists hoped to gain from the political reorganization and realignment which many came to regard as inevitable. In this sense the Fourth of July explosion in the Omaha Coliseum in 1892 was but the opening salvo of the battle of '96. The People's party did, in fact, become a significant force in the political struggles that lay ahead.

At the same time, Populist weaknesses were perhaps even more important than Populist strength. Those weaknesses which became so decisive in 1896 were manifest also in 1892. In the South there was the evident futility of trying to overcome one-party rule and the racial prejudice on which it was based. In the cities there was the problem of trying to attract labor votes with a program that was set up by farmers and agrarians. Within the party there were divisive debates over such controversial issues as the subtreasury. Between farmers in the West and those in the South there were the same commodity conflicts which had worked against union under the Alliance banner.

The Alliance itself was now a thing of the past; the People's party had destroyed it. Disappointed in exchanges and other cooperative economic efforts, Alliancemen had turned to those who promised greater rewards through political action. "The Alliance is nonpartisan, and does not interfere with the political affiliations of its members," insisted *The National Economist*, organ of the Southern Alliance, as delegates gathered at Omaha for the People's party convention. Yet even *The Economist* had to admit that "no longer can any man claim devotion to the demands of the Alliance and consistently affiliate with the Democratic or the Republican parties." Alliancemen had been compelled to join the new party "for conscience sake." Now the People's party would go on to follow a policy of compromise with the old parties—and it would be destroyed. There were elements of classical tragedy in the Populist fate. Having slain its father, the party would now itself be slain.

IV

THE POLITICS OF DEPRESSION

IN THE YEAR 1890 YOUNG WILLIAM ALLEN WHITE WAS living in Eldorado, Kansas, and working as editor of the Eldorado *Republican.* With his salary of $18 a week he could afford to be something of a man about town. Certainly he thought of himself as a member of the ruling class. After a day's work he would sometimes put on a black and gold blazer, white trousers, and black sash and go out to watch the local gentry play tennis. Then as the summer twilight faded into night, he would accompany them to Mort Wells' ice-cream salon. Or sometimes he would tuck a mandolin under his arm and enjoy a night of serenading with equally romantic and well-bred companions. The young editor found Kansas a land of pure delight.

Others, however, did not find it all so idyllic. When the Farmers' Alliance began to organize the county, White was inclined to laugh. After all, this was probably just another of those farmers' cooperatives, a venture that would last perhaps two or three years and then evaporate in the hot prairie sun. Yet when the Alliance held its county convention, the courthouse was filled to overflowing. Its very size, symbolized for White by "a dado of backsides sticking out of the courtroom windows," disturbed for a moment the complacency of the honorable gentlemen who ruled the county. Nevertheless *Republican* editorials jeered at the uprising. Only later could White see that the day of prosperity—the day of the great industrial boom—was drawing to a close. "Those rumps of seedy farmers sticking out of the Courthouse window in Eldorado, Butler County, Kansas, as the Farmers' Alliance county convention met, cast the shadows of a great twilight," recalled the editor some fifty years later. "In another three years came the night—the collapse, and the depression of '93."

One by one the ominous signs began to multiply, not just in Kansas but throughout the world. From London in the fall of 1890 came reports of the collapse of the Barings, international bankers whose services to the British Empire the Queen had many times formally recognized. Although the Bank of England came to the rescue, European financial institutions felt the shock. So did those in the United States. For several months crop failures in Europe and bumper crops in America combined to assure prosperity as grains were exported at high prices. Then, shortly after Grover Cleveland moved into the White House in 1893, came the day of reckoning. On May 3 the stock market collapsed. The next day the National Cordage Company was in the hands of receivers, and three Wall Street brokerage houses failed.

All this was only a beginning. Early in the year men had looked to a future bright with hope. The Chicago world's fair, they thought, would bring tourists into the country and stimulate trade. But the day of the fair's opening came and went without signs of increase in either tourism or trade. "It is easy now to admit that the expectation was unwarranted," commented the New York *Tribune*, "but the disappointment is none the less." As weeks dragged by, newspapers monotonously announced bankruptcy after bankruptcy. "The failure of Schaffner & Co. and the Grant Locomotive Works at Chicago, the Plankinton Bank at Milwaukee, the Victoria Cordage Company at Cincinnati and the Domestic Sewing Machine Company here," intoned the New York *Tribune* in June, "each supposed to have liabilities reckoned in the millions, besides 236 other failures in the

United States alone, indicate clearly the financial pressure." At the same time wheat in Chicago was selling at the lowest price in thirty years.

The year set a record for bank failures; there were some 583 of them, if loan and trust companies and mortgage companies are included. This of course meant severe financial and commercial dislocation. Most of the failures were in the South and West, yet the problem was of more than local concern. Faced with crisis, interior banks withdrew funds from New York banks, and those withdrawals affected not only New York reserves but the stock market as well. Cause led to effect and effect in turn became cause. In all, close to 16,000 businesses failed by the end of the year.

No segment of society escaped the disaster of 1893. Henry Adams, called back to Boston from Switzerland because of the precarious state of his own affairs, found a financial maelstrom. "Everyone is in a blue fit of terror," he observed, "and each individual thinks himself more ruined than his neighbor." In December Samuel Gompers of the American Federation of Labor estimated the number of unemployed at three million. Times were not actually that bad, but they were bad enough. New York City police counted almost 70,000 unemployed and 20,000 homeless and vagrant. In Chicago the Columbian Exposition attracted vagrants as well as sightseers. Reports had it that 100,000 persons in the city were out of work during the winter of 1893-1894. Policemen were detailed to railroad stations to keep out transients, and still they came.

Integration of isolated figures provides some idea of the depression's intensity. Available statistics on production and business activities indicate a fluctuation of about one-fourth from high to low during the decade. In other words, during the worst months of the nineties the economy was functioning at 25 per cent below capacity. Portrayed graphically, economic activity shows peaks in July, 1890, January, 1893, December, 1895, and June, 1899. Troughs came in May, 1891, June, 1894, and June, 1897. The decline in 1891 was quite mild and recovery rapid. By contrast the drop in 1893-1894 was sharp. The recovery of 1895 was both partial and short-lived, as once again the economy succumbed to downward pressures in 1896 and 1897. In mid-summer, 1897, there were indications of an upward turn. "Wheat sold at $1 per bushel today—the highest price since 1891," noted Charles G. Dawes in his diary on August 21. "Prosperity seems to be dawning at last." The observation was correct in its essentials, but there was as yet little cause for rejoicing. Full recovery would not come until well after the turn of the century.

Men were baffled by the depression of the nineties. Living in a period when the secular trend was toward ever greater economic capacity, they had to face the frustrations of accounting for setbacks. It was no easy task, and perhaps it is no wonder that all contemporary explanations contained elements of oversimplification. Grasping a part of the truth, prophets stepped forth to plead for this or that course of action. And of course the crisis produced quacks who grasped no truth at all save that there was a crisis.

Even respected economists, frequently resorting to analogy, failed to explain what had happened. The alternate periods of good times and bad in the nineteenth century were compared to the swing of a pendulum. The depression was likened to a storm; if one weathered it, clear skies would bring prosperity. Or the depression was a disease which weakened the nation. Until deep-seated troubles in the circulatory or nervous system of the economy were relieved, a return to buoyancy and health was impossible. Such verbalisms perhaps masked an ignorance of what was going on, but by no means did they inhibit discussion. On the contrary, citizens engaged in what was to become one of the great public debates in American history.

Agrarian radicals in the West and South pointed accusing fingers at Wall Street and the money power. Some of them saw in the depression a conspiracy to ruin the farmer and seize his land. Others complained of low prices, high freight rates, lack of credit, inadequate currency, and unsympathetic public officials. Samuel Gompers spoke for workingmen when he said that the panic would have been averted or at least made less intense had any attention been paid to labor's demands for shorter working hours. At its convention in Chicago the American Federation of Labor adopted a resolution declaring that "the right to work is the right to live," and that "when the private employers cannot or will not give work, the municipality, State or Nation must." Preachers of the Social Gospel emphasized the economic implications in the message of Jesus. Disciples of Henry George saw basic evils in unearned land values and urged the single tax panacea. Throughout the country National Clubs, inspired by Edward Bellamy, discussed the iniquities of nineteenth-century capitalism and the possibilities of collectivism.

A few observers, most of them on the conservative side of economic questions, attributed the depression to industrial overproduction. Domestic markets, they argued, were unable to absorb all that American manufacturers were producing. If this analysis was correct, then an obvious solution to bad times would be to find markets abroad. For the most part, however, conservative defenders of property were not yet ready to accept the theory of industrial overproduction and all that it implied. Instead, they concentrated on maintaining the gold standard against a double peril. On the one hand, Populists and monetary reformers were demanding the free and unlimited coinage of silver and an increase in the stock of money. On the other, as American and foreign investors began to doubt the government's ability to maintain gold convertibility, the Treasury's gold reserve was subjected to unusual pressure. Thus it was easy and natural for conservatives to blame radical disturbances for a weakening of confidence in the American economy and to see here a major cause of the depression.

If agrarian and other radicals sometimes felt themselves unjustifiably scorned and reviled, conservatives at times also exhibited sensitivity to unfounded accusations. *Harper's Weekly*, for example, was distressed by a tendency to regard Wall Street as "a dark, mysterious, crafty, wicked, rapacious, and tyrannical power—a power that seeks to rob and oppress and enslave the people, and to sweep all the wealth of the country into its own insatiable maw." In September, 1893, the magazine argued that such a view obscured the arguments against free silver. To the silverite, "the Eastern business community and 'Wall Street' are one and the same thing—a lot of greedy capitalists who want to grind the 'debtor class' to powder, and to that end conspire to make money scarce and dear." It was conceded that Wall Street financiers were by no means self-sacrificing philanthropists. They were shrewd businessmen keenly alive to their own interests. And this was precisely the point: shrewd businessmen do not plot to undermine prosperity. "The Wall Street financiers are as much interested in having *plenty of money* in circulation as the rest of the country," concluded the editorial. "And the rest of the country is as much interested in having *good money* in circulation as are the Wall Street financiers."

Discussions of the depression pitted the urban East against the rural West and South, the conservative against the radical, and labor against capital. Political parties were also active in the great debate, although it was some time before they made much of a contribution to it. Quite naturally Democrats blamed Republicans for the panic because Republican legislation was still in effect when the panic began. Republicans, however, had the better of it; fortunately for the GOP the Democrats were in office when the panic deepened into depression. Furthermore, contended the Republicans, the reckless campaign talk about reducing the tariff frightened the business community and contributed to a loss of confidence.

Ultimately, however, the debate centered on the money question. All other considerations—the overexpansion and faulty financing of railroads, the problem of agricultural and industrial overproduction, the European depression—all the causes or suggested causes of depression were subordinated to the discussion of silver and gold coinage. The money issue was no Johnny-come-lately among the questions of the day. Indeed, much of the economic history of the nineteenth century cannot be understood without proper attention to money matters. Yet never before, not even in Andrew Jackson's time, did the money issue assume a place of such overriding importance in the popular mind.

Why did the money question become so important? One reason was that for more than forty years after the Civil War prices declined steadily. Of course the rate of decline was not the same for all goods. In the 1870's prices of producer durables fell more rapidly than did prices for farm products, probably because technological developments in manufacturing made cheaper production possible. But when the panic of 1893 came, farm prices were declining more rapidly. In any case, the long period of deflation was hard on farmers with shrinking incomes, on workers who lost jobs during depressions made more severe by the downward movement of prices, and on debtors who were hard pressed to meet their obligations.

Those who hoped to organize such men in support of relief measures posited a direct correlation between prices and the amount of money in circulation. Scarce or dear money meant low prices and economic contractions. Declining prices required debtors to pay back more in terms of volume of commodities than had been borrowed. Gold was dear and it was deflationary. Gold monometallism, ran the silver argument, could not sustain price levels because it could not provide the country with an adequate circulating medium. This was the central issue, as Nevada Senator William M. Stewart saw it. "The inevitable ruin which must follow the continued contraction which the gold standard is producing and will continue to produce can not be endured by an intelligent people," he wrote William Jennings Bryan. Gold would have to be supplemented with silver.

Advocates of both gold and silver believed that free coinage of silver would have an inflationary effect. But silver men contended that some inflation would restore monetary stability and speed the return of prosperity. Or, to use terminology that had a more direct appeal to debt-ridden farmers of the West and South, silver would arrest the price decline and would enable debtors to meet their obligations. Defenders of the gold standard, on the other hand, argued that silver inflation was unjust. Any inflation would cheat creditors, persons living on fixed incomes, and workers whose wages would lag behind prices.

Whether or not silverites would eventually carry the day for free coinage—and they came close to victory in the nineties—almost constant pressure for inflationary currency characterized the entire period of deflation after the Civil War. During the war itself the government had printed fiat paper money, or greenbacks. After the war there was much agitation from "soft-money" men to increase the greenbacks in circulation, but in 1875 Congress passed the Resumption Act. That act provided that after January 1, 1879, the government would maintain convertibility between greenbacks and gold. Greenbacks would be as good as gold, and the United States was placed on a *de facto* gold standard.

Other financial legislation in the seventies had far-reaching political consequences. In 1873 the silver dollar was omitted from the coinage lists because no one was bringing silver into the mint. With the coinage ratio at 16 to 1 (16 parts silver to 1 of gold) silver was worth more in the market than at the mint. The discovery and development of new mines in the West greatly altered the situation, however, as American silver production quadrupled between 1870 and 1890. The price of silver fell in international markets, and when it did a great hue and cry went up for a return to silver coinage at the old ratio. By 1896 a silver dollar—had it been coined at 16 to 1 and not backed by gold—would have contained an amount of silver worth 53 cents on the market. But long before that, inflationists joined with western silver producers in condemning the "Crime of '73."

So great was the influence of the silver inflationists that in 1878 Congress passed the Bland-Allison Act, which authorized silver coinage in limited amounts. The Secretary of the Treasury was instructed to buy not less than $2 million and not more than $4 million worth of silver each month at the market price. Even though the minimum amount was purchased during the next dozen years, the Treasury's monetary silver by 1890 came to almost $380 million.

At this point, Republicans were seeking support for the McKinley tariff bill. In return for the votes of silver senators, they agreed to further silver legislation, and the Sherman Silver Purchase Act was passed. It differed from the Bland-Allison Act in that it directed the Secretary of the Treasury to purchase monthly 4.5 million ounces of silver bullion. Treasury notes were to be issued in payment for the silver, and they could be redeemed in either gold or silver at the discretion of the government. At 1890 prices the Sherman Act made possible the purchase of almost twice as much silver as did the Bland-Allison Act. Yet the market price of silver continued to fall so rapidly that by 1893 the dollar amount of the monthly purchases was not much greater than it had been under the old act.

The $500 million added to the circulating medium through silver purchases was a substantial victory for advocates of silver. Monetary gold stock also increased during the period after 1875. In the decade of the eighties the quantity of monetary gold doubled. If all types of money including bank deposits are considered, it would seem that the total stock of money kept pace with manufacturing output and national wealth. Production and money supply curves ran roughly parallel in the last quarter of the nineteenth century; in fact from 1860 to 1920 the over-all rate of increase of money supply and of industrial production was about the same. Comparison of the two rates of increase has led many students of the period to conclude that monetary influences had little to do with the business cycle in general or with the depression of the nineties in particular.

How far wrong, then, was the argument of nineteenth-century inflationists that the hard times resulted from a shortage of money? It was discredited of course, and for some time no respectable economist took it seriously. It was never really disproved, however, and in recent studies it has reappeared in much more sophisticated garb than it wore in the nineties.

Milton Friedman, in particular, has suggested that an inadequate rate of growth of the money stock is, if not a complete explanation for business contraction, at least an important consideration. Careful analysis of data, he contends, indicates that the stock of money declined by a significant amount in 1875-1879, 1892-1893, 1895-1896, 1907-1908, 1920-1921, 1929-1933, and 1937-1938. Each of these declines, it is perhaps superfluous to point out, occurred during a severe business contraction. And the list includes all major depressions since the Civil War. Evidently the over-all increase in the stock of money was so marked as to cause other analysts to ignore or minimize declines in the crucial depression years.

Whatever the merits of Friedman's study (these few comments by no means do it justice) most silverites of the nineties attributed their difficulties to a deflationary currency or an inadequate stock of money. Obviously there was more than one monetary question involved in the silver controversy. There was the matter of how much silver to coin. Silver men argued that the limited coinage possible under the Sherman Act was inadequate and pleaded for "free and unlimited coinage" at the ratio of 16 to 1. Then there was the further question of whether or not silver provided the best means of increasing the money supply. Some who were sympathetic to the idea that the stock of money should be expanded were at the same time reluctant to advocate silver.

In January, 1891, the Omaha *World Herald* carried an editorial which argued that free coinage and expansion of the money supply were two entirely separate questions. Free coinage would be "a great thing for those who own silver and silver mines," but it was by no means certain that it would increase the money stock. "Indeed," contended the editorial, "under certain circumstances free coinage might actually mean the lessening of the supply of money by driving out gold." The millions who wanted more money "do not care whether the increase is on gold, silver, greenbacks or certificates as long as it is an increase." Before long, however, silver did win over the advocates of more money including the *World Herald*. Perhaps because it was, after all, a hard metal it had more prestige than paper could command. Even though it would be inflationary if coined in unlimited amounts at 16 to 1, silver was easier to associate with the hard-money predilections of the old Jacksonians. And the law by which silver had been demonetized in 1873 fit nicely into the theory that low prices resulted from a Wall Street conspiracy.

However attractive silver might have been to some, it held no charms for Grover Cleveland. A zealous defender of the gold standard, he blamed the Sherman Silver Purchase Act for the depression.

The Treasury purchases, he reasoned, had encouraged speculation and had raised serious doubts about United States monetary policy. Uncertainty had aroused fears among those hoarding gold and among foreign investors who withdrew gold from the country. Withdrawals and hoarding, combined with an unfavorable balance of trade in 1893, created serious problems for the Treasury. The policy of redeeming all Treasury notes in gold would soon be impossible without statutory changes.

The logic of Cleveland's doctrine allowed only one course of action. Since the nation's economic misfortunes resulted from the Sherman Silver Purchase Act, the only thing to do was to repeal the act. Accordingly, Congress was called into special session on August 7, 1893. The President's message pointed out that between July 1, 1890, and July 15, 1893, the gold coin and bullion in the Treasury decreased by more than $132 million. At the same time, silver coin and bullion increased more than $147 million. Clearly the end of the gold standard and of civilization was in sight unless Congress repealed the loathsome act.

No political leader ever acted with more constancy than Grover Cleveland displayed during those trying summer months in 1893. Shortly before Congress convened, the President had a cancerous growth removed from the roof of his mouth. Performed in secrecy aboard a yacht in New York harbor, the operation proved successful. Cleveland was equipped with an artificial jaw of vulcanized rubber, and he carried on with his duties as though nothing had happened.

The President's stoicism in facing his illness was matched by his willingness to face the political consequences of his recommendations to Congress. He knew full well that members of his own party from the South and West differed with him on the causes of the depression. *The Literary Digest* in July had conducted a poll of newspapers on the advisability of repeal. Replies indicated that 125 out of 175 editors favored unconditional repeal. If the poll showed anything, it showed that Cleveland could count on newspaper support. Yet newspaper opinion and public opinion are not necessarily the same thing. There was certain to be a protest against repeal of the purchase clauses, and there was a strong possibility that it would split the Democratic party. Nevertheless the President refused to compromise.

The silver debate reached its climax on August 16, when Cleveland's proposal was answered in the House of Representatives by the young congressman from Nebraska, William Jennings Bryan. For three hours he held the floor, reiterating arguments men had heard before in a manner that defied comparison with any previous statement. Bryan was dramatic: "In the princely palace and in the humblest hamlet; by the financier and by the poorest toiler; here, in Europe, and everywhere, the proceedings of this Congress upon this problem will be read and studied; and as our actions bless or blight we shall be commended or condemned." He was witty: "The poor man is called a socialist if he believes that the wealth of the rich should be divided among the poor, but the rich man is called a financier if he devises a plan by which the pittance of the poor can be converted to his use." He was erudite: he quoted from economists and public officials on both sides of the money question. He was righteously vehement, like the Old Testament prophets he sometimes cited:

> The President has recommended unconditional repeal. It is not sufficient to say that he is honest—so were the mothers who with misguided zeal threw their children into the Ganges. The question is not 'Is he honest?' but 'Is he right?' He won the confidence of the toilers of this country because he taught that 'public office is a public trust,' and because he convinced them of his courage and his sincerity. But are they willing to say, in the language of Job, 'Though He slay me, yet will I trust Him?' Whence comes this irresistible demand for unconditional repeal? Are not the representatives here as near to the people and as apt to know their wishes? Whence comes the demand? Not from the workshop and the farm, not from the workingmen of this country, who create its wealth in time of peace and protect its flag in time of war, but from the middle-men, from what are termed the 'business interests,' and largely from that class which can force Congress to let it issue money at a pecuniary profit to itself if silver is abandoned. The President has been deceived. He can no more judge the

wishes of the great mass of our people by the expressions of these men than he can measure the ocean's silent depths by the foam upon its waves.

Despite his eloquence Bryan was unsuccessful. The inflationists tried to substitute a free silver bill for the administration bill and were defeated. Then the House voted on August 28 to repeal the Sherman law. The vote, standing 239 to 108, was an overwhelming victory, though ultimately a hollow one, for the President. In the Senate the vote was more evenly divided and the struggle correspondingly more bitter. Filibustering silver senators did their best to talk the repeal bill to death, and they very nearly succeeded. At one point even the staunchest Cleveland Democrats were ready to compromise with the silverites. But Cleveland himself would not listen. Almost ruthless in his use of the patronage, he stolidly pursued his objective. Finally on October 30 he got what he wanted when the Senate voted to repeal the Sherman Act, 43 to 32.

The President had achieved victory at the cost of party unity. As there was no compromise in Cleveland's attitude, so silver men accepted the alternatives as they found them. In August Bryan had said that the Democratic party stood between two great forces. On one side were "the corporate interests of the nation, its moneyed institutions, its aggregations of wealth and capital, imperious, arrogant, compassionless." On the other side stood "that unnumbered throng which gave a name to the Democratic party and for which it has assumed to speak." To describe the forces was to ask which the party would choose to follow. In his peroration Bryan had changed the metaphor but not the question. The party, he said, had in 1892 won the greatest success in its history. "Standing upon this victory-crowned summit, will it turn its face to the rising or the setting sun?" Which would it choose, he asked, life or death, blessings or cursings?

Some historians have criticized Cleveland for forcing the issue as he did. Several of his closest advisors thought at the time that he should have been more equivocal and more ambiguous. Certainly he could have been more tactful. So he has been called dogmatic and shortsighted, pigheaded and inept. Was it obstinacy, incompetence, or courage that led him to stake everything on repeal of the Sherman Act? That is precisely what he did when he blamed silver purchases for the depression. Now if repeal did not bring recovery, his position would be exceedingly awkward. Cleveland had burned his bridges behind him.

The silver question divided the country as had nothing else since the Civil War. In commenting on the action of Congress in repealing the Sherman Act, the Denver *News* said that the chief significance of the vote lay in its sectional character. The paper pointed out that except for Cameron of Pennsylvania all senators from northern states east of the Missouri River voted for repeal. Of the eighteen Democratic votes against repeal, all but three were southern. Of the eight Republican votes, all except Cameron's were from silver-producing states. All five Populist votes against repeal came from the West, and three of those were from silver-producing states. "The lesson is a plain one," observed the *News*. "All the great States of the East, the Middle States and those of the Northeast are welded in a solid body to destroy silver as primary money. The States of the South and the entire West between the Pacific Ocean and the Missouri River are solid for restoring silver to its old status as primary money and giving it free coinage with gold at the mints." The issue split both Republican and Democratic parties on sectional lines, but the break in Democratic ranks had more sensational consequences. Perhaps because the Democrats were in power, every question that came up served to widen the breach. By 1896 it was impassable.

The worst that can be said about Cleveland's policy, however, is that it failed to achieve the results he predicted. The nation waited in vain for relief. There were signs of an upswing during November, but as the Philadelphia *Record* admitted, "the progress of betterment is disappointingly slow." Prices and wages showed little if any improvement. Unemployment remained high. And most alarming of all, the depletion of gold reserves in the Treasury continued at a rapid rate.

For years financiers and Treasury Department officials had regarded a gold reserve of at least $100 million as the *sine qua non* of sound fiscal policy. Even before President Harrison left office, the gold reserve had begun to decline. It had long since sunk below the magic $100 million mark. On the day the Senate voted to repeal the Sherman Act, the gold reserve stood at $84 million. By the end of 1893 it was at $80 million. During the gloomy January of 1894, the reserve fell to a new low of $62 million. Obviously the administration would have to act.

Secretary of the Treasury John G. Carlisle decided in December to ask Congress for authority to float short-term loans at low interest rates. Silverites, who saw no reason why bonds should be sold for gold when Treasury Department vaults held plenty of silver, blocked the Carlisle proposal. When $11 million in gold left the Treasury during the first half of January, Cleveland exclaimed to his cabinet, "This don't [*sic*] help us. I believe in taking the bull by the horns and coming out with an issue of bonds." Accordingly on January 17, Carlisle sent out a circular announcing the sale of 4 per cent bonds to the amount of $50 million. Payment was to be made in gold, and no bids would be accepted at less that 117.223, which would put the bonds on a 3 per cent basis. Banks and financiers applauded the action, but they were slow in buying bonds. It took a meeting with administration men to arouse their patriotism to the point where the bond sale was assured.

Like the repeal of the Sherman Act, the bond issue could be criticized on two grounds: it was not effective, and it was politically ill-advised. It was ineffective because some $24 million was withdrawn from the Treasury by subscribers who redeemed notes in order to pay for the bonds in gold. It was a political bungle because it further alienated the West and South. It confirmed the silverites in their suspicions that the administration was deeply involved in a conspiracy against the people. "The Presidents of the United States and their secretaries of finance," said Bryan's friend, Populist Senator William V. Allen of Nebraska, "have been and are now fastened by golden cords to a combination of the worst men in the world."

Having resorted once to bonds, the Cleveland administration saw no alternative but to continue the policy with another issue as gold reserves continued to decline. The second bond issue, somewhat more successful than the first, helped to bring the reserve up to $111 million by December. To silver men it seemed that government bonds were a drug on the market and that Cleveland was addicted to it. Yet both Cleveland and Carlisle recognized the limitations of action the Treasury was taking. In his annual message the President said, "We have an endless chain in operation constantly depleting the Treasury's gold and never near a final rest." He went on, however, to suggest that it was all really the fault of Congress because that body had "thus far declined to authorize the issue of bonds best suited to such purpose." Grover Cleveland was not one to cry *mea culpa.*

During the months of December, 1894, and January, 1895, the monotonous story of gold withdrawals repeated itself. By February 8 the reserve had declined to less than $42 million. Cleveland asked Congress for power to cancel notes as they came in for redemption and for legislation to require the payment of import duties in gold. He was turned down. So there seemed nothing to do but issue more bonds. This time no circulars went out. Instead the matter was discussed privately with J. P. Morgan and August Belmont, who agreed to purchase $62 million in 4 per cent bonds at 104½. This provided the Treasury with something more than $65 million worth of gold. The bankers further agreed to secure half the gold from abroad and to do what they could to protect the government against further withdrawals. Once the deal was consummated, Morgan and Belmont lost no time in disposing of the bonds—at what profits to themselves no one ever found out.

Standard pro-Cleveland or "sound-money" accounts of the Treasury crisis give it the coloring of an old-fashioned melodrama with silverites playing villains' roles. The advocates of silver of course did not see it that way at all. If anyone doubted after the signing of the Morgan-Belmont contract that goldbugs were a sinister influence in American life, then he was not at heart a silverite. Cleveland rejected all suggestion of conciliation with silver forces (he even vetoed a bill to coin the silver seigniorage), but he was actually proud of his part in the negotiations with Morgan and Belmont. "What is this contract?" an outraged Bryan asked rhetorically in the House of Representatives. "It is a contract made by the Executive of a great nation with the representatives of foreign money loaners. It is a contract made with men who are desirous of changing the financial policy of this country." The President had broken faith with the American people. He had also betrayed the Democratic party. Any gratitude party members might feel toward Cleveland would be "the gratitude which a passenger feels toward the trainman who has opened a switch and precipitated a wreck."

Meanwhile, throughout much of the controversy over money, the Cleveland administration struggled with the tariff reform promised during the campaign of 1892. In a major revision such as had been contemplated, problems were perhaps unavoidable. "Tariff reform may be useful as a campaign slogan, but it becomes a general assault upon the industries of the country when it is embodied in legislation," noted the Baltimore *American*. "And these industries can arouse a rather formidable opposition when their interests are attacked." Nevertheless Cleveland considered his election a mandate for revision, and soon after repeal of the Sherman Silver Purchase Act the tariff was taken up in the House.

From the administration's point of view Congress started out well enough. A bill approved by Cleveland was reported to the House by Congressman William L. Wilson just before Christmas 1893, and it passed in February the following year. It won the support of most low tariff men including Bryan. The measure as passed by the House would have reduced the average rates from almost 50 per cent to about 30 per cent on dutiable goods. At the same time, the Wilson bill placed many raw materials—including wool, coal, iron ore, hemp, and flax—on the free list. The theory behind the provision was that free raw materials would permit lower production costs for American manufacturers and therefore facilitate penetration of world markets for industrial goods. "We could throw down to-day our tariff walls and defy the world's competition," said Wilson in support of this new approach to prosperity. Another unusual feature of the bill (one which Cleveland approved with reluctance) was one providing for a 2 per cent tax on incomes of over $4,000. This, wrote reform-minded Senator Roger Q. Mills, "is but a light touch on the monumental piles of wealth, for the protection of which the government is standing guard."

It was in the Senate that the administration's tariff program met with overpowering resistance. That particular interests should assert themselves in opposition to particular measures was to be expected. Some senators opposed free raw materials, and others the income tax; some opposed the bill out of spite, for the President did have enemies. Yet tariff measures are not notable for their neat, logical symmetry, and there was room for compromise and accommodation. Instead of placating Senator Gorman and other protectionist Democrats, however, Cleveland attacked their disloyalty. Since he had used most of his patronage power to secure an end to silver purchases, this was hardly the time for verbal assaults on fellow Democrats. In any case the President lost his chance to effect a satisfactory compromise.

The measure finally passed by the Senate in July and approved by the House in August was a far cry from the tariff reform which had been sought. So displeased was the President, especially with elimination of the free list, that he refused to sign the bill, and it became law without his signature. Only the discerning could see much difference between the Wilson-Gorman tariff of 1894 and the McKinley tariff of 1890. True, the act of 1894 contained provision for an income tax, a measure which had long seemed attractive to tax reformers and which had been included in the Populist platform. But that innovation came to nothing, for in May, 1895, the Supreme Court declared it unconstitutional.

On the day the House gave its final approval to the Wilson-Gorman tariff, Cleveland described himself as "a man depressed and disappointed." There was ample justification for such a mood. As politicians prepared for the congressional elections of 1894, the President had little to show for his efforts during seventeen months in office. Repeal of the Sherman Silver Purchase Act did not reverse the downward curve of the business cycle. The vexing problem of the gold reserve was no nearer solution than it had been at the time of the first bond issue. The attempt to secure tariff reform had failed.

The administration's monetary policy had split the Democratic party. While most Republicans supported Cleveland in the struggle to maintain the gold standard, they did not forget partisan politics. They continued to blame the Democrats for the depression, arguing that discussion of lower tariff duties had paralyzed business. After the passage of the new tariff act, they continued this line of attack. They could then contend that the President placed effect before cause in attributing the depression to the outflow of gold instead of to the deficiency of revenue. By 1896 the staunchly Republican Omaha *Bee* was saying, "The whole financial trouble, so far as the national treasury is concerned, is due to the fact that the income of the government, under the operation of the democratic tariff, has been less than the outgo, the deficiency being supplied by borrowing." There was sophistry in the argument, but it was effective in winning votes.

If all this were not enough, 1894 brought troubles of another kind. As the depression deepened, signs of unrest began to appear. With increasing unemployment came a series of strikes, and some of the jobless joined wandering industrial armies which appeared mainly in the West. Men of property began to be haunted by the spectre of revolution.

The industrial armies, of which Jacob S. Coxey's was the most famous, attracted much attention during the spring and summer as they made their way—a "petition in boots"—to the nation's capital. What did these men want? Most of them simply wanted jobs, but Coxey himself had some idea of using the unemployed to build good roads. The costs would be met with legal-tender notes issued by the Secretary of the Treasury. Coxey recruited his followers from his home in Massillon, Ohio, but most of the armies came from the Pacific Coast and Mountain areas, and they arrived in Washington at different times during 1894. There the movement petered out. In what developed into a fiasco, Coxey and other leaders of his army were arrested; they were convicted of carrying banners on the Capitol grounds and of walking on the grass.

If there had only been the marches of industrial armies to report during that summer of 1894, the men of property might have rested somewhat easier. As it was, a series of events in Chicago shocked the nation and aroused new anxieties. The trouble began with a dispute between George M. Pullman and the workers in his Pullman Palace Car Company. Just south of Chicago, Pullman had built a company town which came as close to being a feudal estate as was possible in an industrial age. There he housed his workers and their families, and there railroad cars of all descriptions were manufactured. Despite the depression the company did well enough to pay $2,880,000 in dividends in 1894. At the same time, however, the wages of workers were cut on five different occasions while the high rents in Pullman were maintained. Reaching the point of desperation some 4,000 workers joined the American Railway Union and sent a grievance committee to treat with the lord of the manor. He refused to listen. On May 11, after three members of the unsuccessful deputation were discharged, the workers called a strike.

The dispute soon developed into a showdown battle between the American Railway Union, led by Eugene V. Debs, and the Railway Managers' Association, which had been organized eight years earlier by the heads of twenty-four railroads. At the A.R.U. convention in June, Debs urged caution. But members voted to boycott Pullman cars and to close shops at St. Louis and at Ludlow, Kentucky, if the company did not agree to arbitration by June 26. When that day came with no word from Pullman, trains carrying his cars were sidetracked. The railroads, with the Railway Managers' Association supervising operations, then began to fire switchmen who refused to handle Pullman cars. The union retaliated, calling a strike against the railroads. By the end of June one of the most devastating strikes in the nineteenth century had tied up traffic throughout the country.

The resourceful General Managers' Association was not to be thwarted by striking workmen. When workers refused to move Pullman cars, the railroads refused to run trains. This meant that government intervention could be justified on grounds that the strike interfered with the movement of mail. With the assistance of the Managers' Association, government lawyers drew up an injunction which enjoined the union from obstructing the mails. Richard Olney, Cleveland's Attorney General, made his contribution to the cause of peace and order when he suggested a novel interpretation of the Sherman Anti-Trust Act. The strike could be broken, he said, because it was a combination in restraint of trade.

After the injunction was served, a riot occurred in the railroad yards at a Chicago suburb, Blue Island, on July 2. Cars were tipped over and traffic impeded. It was the first act of violence, but it was enough to serve as a pretext for sending Federal troops to Chicago. Most students of the dispute agree that calm had returned to Chicago after the Blue Island riots and that there was no need to call in the United States Army. State officials had not asked for any assistance; there was every reason to believe that state troops were competent to handle any disturbances that might occur. Nevertheless so eager was Olney to break the strike that orders went out to Fort Sheridan, and Army forces entered the city.

The arrival of United States troops caused a violent reaction. Windows were smashed, buildings were fired, cars were overturned, twelve people were killed. How much of the property damage was attributable to the American Railway Union is still an open question, but at no time did Debs or the Union urge the use of violence. After an uneasy week the strike was broken. The A.R.U. simply did not have the funds to carry on the fight against both the railroads and the Federal government. The union's members were blacklisted, and it lost its influence. Labor unions in general were imperiled when the Supreme Court upheld the use of the injunction as justified by Olney.

The Cleveland administration paid dearly for restoring order to

Chicago. Debs went to jail and acquired a martyr's following. Not yet persuaded by socialist doctrines to which he listened with increasing sympathy, he emerged to support silver and Bryan in 1896. But for the moment a far more important figure was John Peter Altgeld. The son of German immigrants, he had enjoyed considerable business success before his election as governor of Illinois in 1892. He was the first Democrat to hold that office since the Civil War, but his party affiliations did not prevent him from protesting vigorously the sending of Federal troops into Chicago. So deep was his sense of outrage that he became a leader in the anti-Bourbon wing of the Democracy. None of Grover Cleveland's enemies figured more prominently in the movement which resulted in repudiation of the President by his own party in 1896.

Had Cleveland deliberately set out to antagonize fellow Democrats, he could hardly have been more successful. "I hate the ground the man walks on," said Senator John T. Morgan of Alabama. Congressional elections have seldom been held under conditions less auspicious for the party in power. "The Democratic mortality will be so great next fall that their dead will be buried in trenches and marked 'unknown,'" Tom Reed prophesied early in 1894. Later, as crisis followed crisis and opposition to Cleveland built up, Reed embellished his remark: "until the supply of trenches gives out." To an unusual degree national issues were a factor in state and local elections.

State elections in 1893 had already given some inkling of the drift of public opinion. In eight northern states which the parties had divided in 1892, the Republicans were victorious. Yet the fact of their victory was perhaps less impressive than an increase of more than 340,000 in net plurality. The movement away from the Democratic party was demonstrated even more strikingly in 1894. Champ Clark of Missouri described the Democratic rout that year as the greatest slaughter of the innocents since Herod.

Analysis of the vote by sections indicates that the impact of the depression rocked the country and that voters did not agree with

Cleveland's program for overcoming it. The Northeast—including the New England states, New York, New Jersey, and Pennsylvania—elected 92 Republicans and 7 Democrats to the House of Representatives. Only Boston's John Fitzgerald was successful among New England Democrats. Five of the other Democratic victors came from New York City and one from Pennsylvania. In 1892 the Democrats had won 44 seats from these northeastern states. The most sensational losses were in New York and New Jersey. The number of Democratic congressmen from New York dropped from 19 to 5, while the number of Republicans elected to the House increased from 15 to 29. New Jersey for the first time elected a solid Republican group of congressmen. Legislatures in all the northeastern states went Republican, and Republicans were successful in every gubernatorial contest. Where members of the GOP were re-elected, their pluralities were greater in 1894 than they had been in 1892.

The Republican tide swept into the Middle West with devastating force. In the five states of the Old Northwest where the Democrats had elected 44 congressmen in 1892, they were now able to elect only 3. The number of Republican congressmen from these states increased from 34 to 75. Of the three surviving Democrats, two were from Ohio and one from Illinois. The Populists did not do as well in these states as had been expected, polling less than 8 per cent of the vote and failing to elect any of their candidates.

In the prairie and plains states between the Mississippi and the Rockies it was pretty much the same story. Although the Populists were more important there, they did not do as well as they had in 1892 when they joined with Democrats in criticizing the Harrison administration. In 1894, however, there was not much fusion in the West; Populists opposed the policies of Cleveland as vigorously as did any Republicans. The seven states north of Arkansas and the Indian Territory sent 44 Republicans, 4 Democrats, and 2 Populists to the House of Representatives. In the elections for state offices the Republicans had things as much their own way as they did in the congressional elections. Populist Judge Silas A. Holcomb, who was elected governor of Nebraska, provided the exception to this Republican rule.

In the far West party labels meant little. In its analysis of the election, the *Review of Reviews* observed: "The dominant party in Nevada is neither Republican, Democratic nor Populist; its sole *raison d'etre* is its demand for free silver." The same thing could be said of the entire western coast and Rocky Mountain area. In general the successful candidates were those who campaigned as Republicans, but everybody was for free and unlimited coinage of silver at 16 to 1.

In the South, too, the party label lost some of its meaning, for there was more fusion in that region than in others. It was in North Carolina that fusion was worked most successfully. There a combination of Republicans and Populists managed to gain control of the state. In South Carolina, "Pitchfork Ben" Tillman was almost a party unto himself—and a very successful one at that—even though he never left the Democratic party. In other states of the deep South, neither Republicans nor Populists were able to make much headway against the party of white supremacy. In the states of the upper South, however, Republicans did well. They elected 3 out of 6 congressmen from Maryland, 5 out of 11 from Kentucky, and 4 out of 10 from Tennessee. All four of West Virginia's congressmen were Republicans.

What was the significance of the election of 1894? For the Republicans it was the beginning of an eighteen-year period of dominance in national politics. The GOP triumphed in urban as well as rural areas, capturing nearly every major city in the Northeast. Democrats, on the other hand, suffered their heaviest losses in industrial towns. The depression snapped ethnic ties which bound immigrant working-class wards to the Democratic party. Efforts by Democrats to brand the Republicans as nativists and sympathetic to the American Protective Association had little effect on the outcome of the election.

The Populists, hope springing eternal in their breasts, were not discouraged by their failure to elect as many of their candidates as they had in 1892. They pointed to the fact that they had increased their vote to 1,471,590 (42 per cent over 1892), and some of them looked forward to replacing the badly shattered Democracy as one of the major parties. They had a right to hope.

Finally, and perhaps most importantly, the repudiation of President Cleveland and the Bourbon element within the Democratic party provided a stimulus to other elements of the West and South. Silverites and agrarians now labored to gain control of the organization in order to salvage something from four years of Clevelandism. The struggle within the party would not be an easy one, and even when silver finally won out, there could be no return to the equilibrium of the pre-1894 period. The Democratic party was widely regarded as the party of depression and economic nonsense, and it would be a long time before those scarlet stains could be wiped off the Democratic escutcheon.

V

McKINLEY AND THE GOP

WHEN REPUBLICANS GATHERED IN ST. LOUIS FOR THEIR national convention in June, 1896, they proceeded with dispatch to nominate William McKinley for President. Behind the breathtaking majority he received on the first ballot was a carefully planned and superbly executed campaign for the privilege of heading the ticket in a GOP year. McKinley actually began his quest for the nomination shortly after the Republican national convention in 1892. Clearly one of the most popular leaders in the party, he was in demand as a speaker during Benjamin Harrison's second campaign. The Governor of Ohio did his part, and in serving Harrison, he also served himself. He traveled from Maine to Minnesota, talking earnestly with party leaders as well as to the people. Here and there he let it be known confidentially that he would be available in another four years.

Much as McKinley profited from his extensive tour, both he and his astute manager, Mark Hanna, knew that to become a prophet without honor in his own state would hardly do. From the beginning they concentrated on keeping the Ohio party organization in line. This was difficult, for the ephemeral alliances of Ohio politics did not admit of many certainties. Nevertheless McKinley and Hanna managed to secure the chairmanship of the State Executive Committee for their man, Charles W. F. Dick. An energetic young politician from Akron, Dick had a head for statistics and a knack for methodical organization. As one of Hanna's aides he was to exert influence in the Governor's campaign. Another important assistant was Joseph P. Smith, a former newspaperman, who held a sinecure as state librarian. Even with men like Dick and Smith on the job, however, complete domination of Buckeye Republicans was impossible to maintain. Eventually deals would have to be made with some of the leaders of opposing factions.

In the meantime, McKinley's national prominence was assured when Grover Cleveland defeated Harrison in 1892. Everyone knew that Cleveland sought a downward revision of the tariff. And if there was any policy with which the Major associated himself, it was the tariff the President intended to revise. Had there been no panic in 1893 and no depression, McKinley would still have been a leader against Democratic tariff legislation. As it was, the McKinley tariff could be linked with good times, and the man himself could be touted as "the advance agent of Prosperity."

While the depression provided McKinley with unforeseen political opportunities, it also came close to destroying him. He had endorsed the paper of a friend, Robert L. Walker, to the amount of $17,000. Since Walker had contributed to his congressional campaigns and had upon occasion loaned him money, McKinley was glad to do him a favor. What he did not know was that the Walker tin-plate business rested on the flimsiest of financial foundations, and that the purported renewals he signed obligated him to far more than the original sum he had agreed upon. The house of cards Walker had been building collapsed at the onset of the depression in 1893. McKinley learned of his bankruptcy while en route to New York to make a speech. He caught the first train back to Cleveland and looked up Myron Herrick, a better and closer friend than Walker and a prominent banker. For the greater part of a week McKinley remained in seclusion, an anxious house guest of the Herricks, waiting for all the details of his commitment. The final report showed him in for the astronomic total of $130,000. What was to be done? Herrick together with H. H. Kohlsaat, a wholesale baker and part owner of the Chicago *Inter Ocean,* managed to raise enough to meet the first obligations. But they were unable to keep up with mounting liabilities, and in the end it was Mark Hanna who came to the rescue. He set up a fund to which wealthy friends and associates were (privately, of course) invited to contribute. The response was generous and within a few weeks' time McKinley was in the clear. More heart-warming were the unsolicited gifts of a dollar or two which came in from people who sympathized and wanted to help. Such contributions were all returned, but they indicated the strength of those bonds which united McKinley and plain folks.

Although the depression brought personal embarrassment to McKinley, it made his political battles easier to fight. In the fall of 1893 he won re-election handily. Yet winning another term as Governor, important as that was, was overshadowed by the Republican triumph of 1894. McKinley campaigned vigorously that year. Up and down the land he went, preaching the virtues of protectionism and the evils of the Wilson-Gorman tariff. His efforts, he believed, contributed to the Republican landslide. No doubt they did, but even more important to his future, the recently bankrupt advance agent of prosperity was beginning to appear as the chief spokesman for the GOP and its only logical choice for President.

The national convention was more than a year and a half away, however, and much hard work had to be done if the Major was to take full advantage of his opportunities. At this point Mark Hanna, offering vague excuses about enjoyment of one's last years, retired from active control of his coal and iron business. Although he never mentioned it, the move freed him for full-time service to McKinley's cause. "He had come to a parting of the ways," wrote Herbert Croly. "Politics had become more absorbing than business." Fortunately for McKinley, Hanna changed his field of operations, not his ways. The organizational and administrative skills, the capacity for detail, the pragmatic flexibility which helped to account for his business success were as much in evidence as ever. Now they were devoted to different ends.

The degree to which Hanna was responsible for McKinley's ultimate triumph is difficult to assess. His abilities complemented those of the Governor. A direct telephone line connected the McKinley home in Canton with Hanna's office in Cleveland. Always ready for consultation with the formal, platitudinous, moralistic exemplar of Republicanism and Americanism was the realist who had few thoughts about dignity and decorum except to admire those qualities as they appeared in McKinley. "Together," writes Margaret Leech, "these two made one perfect politician."

As McKinley and Hanna formulated their strategy, they regarded with special solicitude the populous, industrialized area east of the Mississippi and north of the Ohio River Mason-Dixon line. They therefore decided to establish an office in Chicago, and they looked around for someone to take charge there. The man they finally chose was Charles G. Dawes, a young, gawky, politically inexperienced businessman who had just moved to the Windy City from Lincoln, Nebraska. One of the curious ironies of the campaign of 1896 was that Charlie Dawes, whose usefulness to McKinley was as great as that of any other man save Hanna, regarded William Jennings Bryan as one of his close friends. Both Dawes and Bryan had gone to Lincoln in 1887 to practice law. Their offices were in the same building and their houses were only a block apart. Both were members of the Round Table, a discussion group in which they frequently found themselves on opposite sides of the argument. Their life-long friendship withstood differences of opinion, even their differences in 1896.

Given his Chicago assignment in March, 1895, Dawes set to work with a will. In the meantime Mark Hanna had turned to another phase of McKinley's campaign for the party nomination. Nobody expected the Republicans to win many electoral votes in the South, even though Populist activity there had changed conditions considerably. But southern convention delegates figured prominently in the McKinley-Hanna plans. Early in 1895 Hanna rented a house in

Thomasville, Georgia, a little resort town in the southern part of the state, and went down for the winter. To be away from northern snow was pleasant, and Hanna enjoyed himself as he chatted about the political situation with party leaders. In March, when McKinley arrived for a three-week visit, Hanna was the perfect host. He made sure that his southern friends were given a chance to see the Governor—on a well-timed schedule. From all over the South they came to meet briefly in convivial little groups at Hanna's retreat.

Yet it took more than Hanna's hospitality and McKinley's charm to win the southern men. "A National Convention," observed a Louisianian about his fellow Republicans in the South, "was regarded as a kind of 'hog killing time' by or through which they were to be benefited. Instead of ascertaining the wishes of delegates representing States on which the country must rely to elect a President they forced a nomination and then retired to await the distribution of federal patronage, boldly claiming their ability to carry their respective States if furnished sufficient funds." The Louisianian was unfair. The southern men did not wish to force anyone's nomination. They could be persuaded to support a candidate, however, and money lent remarkable force to arguments for such support. But even more important than money—which Hanna doubtless used when he had to—was the strength of the candidate. Because the lifeblood of the southern GOP was Federal patronage, southerners had a vital interest in backing a winner. Hanna's job was to persuade them that McKinley could not be beaten.

Early in May, Hanna met with his men on the scene in Chicago and delivered himself of an optimistic progress report on conditions in the South. Had he known then what was about to happen in Ohio, he perhaps would have been more restrained. The 1895 convention of Ohio Republicans which met at Zanesville was not just another state convention, for its decisions could conceivably have national repercussions. Senator John Sherman was there to preside. Of course Hanna was there. But the presence of Joseph Benson Foraker brought consternation to the Hanna-McKinley camp.

Although former Governor Foraker had not been active in politics of late, he nevertheless wielded substantial power. His political ambitions and career were so similar to those of McKinley that some undercurrent of rivalry was unavoidable; a surface cordiality scarcely hid their mutual distrust. For his part Hanna had suspected Foraker of duplicity in deserting Sherman at a critical moment in the national convention of 1888 and had blamed him for the Senator's failure to secure the nomination. Nothing that happened in Zanesville diminished Hanna's suspicions.

Foraker was the obvious leader of all those who for one reason or another resented McKinley-Hanna domination. Quietly, successfully, he and his followers worked behind the scenes. Although the convention endorsed McKinley for President, Foraker men secured all the important jobs in the state organization; Foraker's candidate, Asa Bushnell, received the gubernatorial nomination; and Foraker himself became the Republican choice for United States senator. The convention was generally interpreted as a rout of McKinley-Hanna forces, and it raised serious doubts about McKinley's mastery over his party. One rhymester widely quoted in the press put into verse what he was sure were McKinley's thoughts:

> Which I wish to remark,
> And my language is plain,
> That for ways that are dark
> And which give me a pain
> Joey Foraker's mighty peculiar. . . .

The Zanesville convention did not prove to be as disastrous to the McKinley cause as some had predicted, nor was Foraker as devious in his dealings with McKinley as he could have been. He kept his word. But the very fact that he gave his word suggested some sort of bargain. After Zanesville McKinley had to come to terms; his only other alternative was to give up thoughts of Ohio's support at St. Louis, and without that he could not get very far. Party harmony in the state clearly served both men. For Foraker there was control of the state organization and a seat in the Senate. For McKinley there was support of his candidacy by the Ohio GOP. Events worked out pretty much along those lines, although McKinley—who had more to lose—was given an anxious moment or two.

Foraker was not McKinley's sole political enemy, but he was the only major party leader with whom McKinley seemed ready to bargain. In the fall of 1895 Hanna conferred with state bosses Matthew S. Quay of Pennsylvania and Thomas C. Platt of New York. They seemed willing to side with McKinley in the convention if the Governor reciprocated with one or two small favors. Among other things, Platt wanted the Treasury Department. When the bosses' terms were reported to McKinley, so the story goes, he spurned them. "If I cannot be President without promising to make Tom Platt Secretary of the Treasury," he is supposed to have said, "I will never be President."

This is the stuff of which laudatory biographies are made. But McKinley certainly had the common sense to see that any such deal if it became known would outrage public opinion. McKinley was not incorruptible. The point is that he thought the bosses' price too high. His need was not so great that he had to pay it, and he did not pay it. McKinley's relationship with Foraker suggests that he was willing to treat with political bosses when he thought that doing so was necessary and could be harmonized with his political ethics.

No one of course knows what McKinley really thought when Hanna told him about the negotiations with Platt and Quay. But he did reject the bosses, and in so doing he forced them to come up with a plan for halting the McKinley bandwagon. They held several meetings in the fall of 1895 and early in 1896 without effectively resolving their dilemma. They could not quite unite in support of any one man, and they decided instead to encourage "favorite son" campaigns in several states. The technique was a traditional one. With it the bosses hoped to keep themselves flexible, seizing the main chance when the opportunity came.

That the opportunity never arrived was not attributable to any dearth of favorite sons. From New England came House Speaker

Thomas B. Reed of Maine. The corpulent parliamentarian with the cynical, razor-sharp mind was more closely identified with sound money and the gold standard than was McKinley. In Pennsylvania Quay declared himself available. Platt chose old Levi P. Morton, who had been elected Governor of New York in the Republican sweep of 1894, as his stalking horse. The septuagenarian Governor was eager for the nomination, but he could hardly have been taken seriously. In Illinois, Senator Shelby M. Cullom offered a humdrum but respectable record and his Lincolnesque physiognomy to the cause. A much more plausible choice was Iowa's William Boyd Allison. Like Morton, however, Allison was an old-timer whose years counted against him. He had helped to nominate Lincoln in Chicago in 1860, and he had been active in public life ever since, usually doing what he could for railroads and big business. Finally, former President Harrison was not to be counted out, at least not until he formally withdrew.

The strategy of the bosses promised much. They believed that Reed would dominate New England and the eastern states and that Allison could hold the West. Allison also had support in the South. Other favorite sons could at least prevent McKinley from taking over large blocs of convention votes. But 1896 was unlike any other election year in American history; tried and true methods did not work out. As the Cleveland administration floundered in its efforts to lick the depression, Americans began to demand a new kind of leadership. They cared little about silly ceremonies: candidates trying to make it appear that they were answering the call of the people, favorite sons acting as though they were serious candidates, and politicians in general refusing to take up real issues for fear of giving offense.

William McKinley was no tribune of the people, standing courageously for a coherent program, but the writhing and maneuvering of the bosses made him look like one. The advance agent of prosperity acquired a new slogan. "McKinley against the bosses" appealed to reform elements within the GOP. It also appealed to the man on the street. In a peculiar way, perhaps in large part without conscious awareness or intent, McKinley's campaign reached far beyond the circles of professional politicians.

The combination against McKinley, in the long run powerless to thwart him, was at least a nuisance. Because of it Hanna sometimes had difficulty in obtaining the support he sought. In February, 1896, for example, James M. Swank, general manager of the American Iron and Steel Association, explained why he could not help the Major. "To Reed, Allison, and Quay this Association is under heavy obligation," he wrote. It would be "an ungracious act in us" if the association entered the field against such men, he continued. "You see that my hands are tied." The McKinley organization was never short of funds, but with several favorite sons in the running Hanna and his closest associates had to bear most of the financial burdens of the preconvention campaign. While the bosses' combine might create some problems, however, the supporters of McKinley never had serious doubts about the outcome. "It is the field against McKinley," noted Charles G. Dawes in his journal on February 17. But he added confidently, "Our man is strong enough to beat the field."

The morale of the McKinley organization, high from the very beginning, rose even higher as conventions in state after state declared for the Governor. Joseph H. Manley, Reed's manager, and the urbane James S. Clarkson, who managed Allison's campaign, proved no match for Hanna. Only Thomas C. Platt displayed the political finesse required to defeat McKinley's nomination. Yet even Platt did not have complete control over New York Republicans, and the united efforts of Platt, Quay, Clarkson, and Manley enticed only a handful of southerners away from McKinley. In the Reed country McKinley's cousin, Will Osborne, had been hard at work. The Major achieved successes in New Hampshire, where both he and Reed were named as acceptable, and in Vermont, where opportunistic Senator Redfield Proctor threw the state's support to him.

Important as other sections were, however, the crucial states in McKinley's quest for the nomination were the North Central States, and there he scored most convincingly. McKinley himself emphasized the importance of the area when he spoke at the Marquette Club in Chicago on Lincoln's birthday. The occasion provided an opportunity to extol the virtues of McKinley as well as those of the martyr President. Joyously, participants raised a litany to Americanism, Republicanism, and McKinleyism. Copies of the Governor's speech (the only one he gave outside Canton in 1896) were printed and distributed by the thousands. All in all the affair was a great triumph, a suitable celebration of victories achieved and victories to come.

At the Ohio convention in March, Foraker could not have been more generous in his praise. It was now time, he said, to redeem the pledge made to McKinley in 1895. He told the delegates: "We owe it to ourselves as well as to him to do it with spirit, to do it with earnestness, to do it with unanimity, to do it in such a manner, in short, as will signify to the whole nation that he has now, and will have at the St. Louis Convention, the united, hearty, cordial, enthusiastic, unqualified support of Ohio." Delegates concurred with sustained applause, and GOP newspapers in the state echoed the sentiment. "McKinley is to have the unwavering support of Ohio for the Presidency," wrote the editor of the Gallipolis *Tribune*. "It is his just due. He is entitled to it by every consideration of party welfare." Foraker later promised to go to St. Louis and make the nominating speech for McKinley. The candidate, always a stickler for form, expressed his gratitude.

Of course Ohio was not the entire Middle West; Allison had Iowa's endorsement, and there were other states to be heard from. But one by one they fell into line behind McKinley during March and April. Wisconsin Republicans under the leadership of a former Reed man, Henry C. Payne, declared for McKinley on March 19, and Minnesotans took similar action the following week. By the end of April only Illinois, Indiana, and Michigan among the North Central States had yet to instruct their delegates. Indiana and Michigan conventions would not be held until May 7, but they were considered safe for McKinley. When Harrison had withdrawn in February, Hanna had dispatched lieutenants to win over Hoosier party leaders. Former Governor Russell Alger, a strong McKinley supporter, seemed to have the situation in Michigan under control. The Illinois convention, therefore, shaped up as the last decisive one before the gathering of GOP clans in St. Louis.

The fight for Illinois tested young Charles Dawes, and he did not fail. Shelby M. Cullom was the favorite-son candidate, but the entire combination against McKinley had an interest in the result. "We must gather up our loins there," Allison's manager had written in December, "for that is the heart of it all." Dawes and his men became increasingly active as the date of the convention approached. "The McKinley forces are organized all over my State," Cullom complained in March. "They have their agents tramping around, organizing McKinley clubs and doing anything in their power to make the State solid for McKinley." What hurt most of all, perhaps, was the effective activity of Dawes' workers in Logan County, Cullom's own district. After Cullom lost the county, he did not have much to bargain with, but he made the attempt. McKinley would not hear of it. The man who had rebuffed Platt and Quay would not mortgage the Presidency to the likes of Shelby Cullom.

Although the results in Illinois districts generally favored McKinley, GOP factions struggled fiercely for control of the state convention in Springfield. Dawes had to beat back a challenge to his authority among the McKinley men as well as negotiate with Cullom's managers on the order of business. At last all was in readiness for April 30—"the critical day" Dawes called it. Cullom supporters introduced a resolution committing delegates to St. Louis to stand by the Senator. The vote was 503 for the resolution and 832 against. The opposition to McKinley collapsed, and the convention proceeded forthwith to instruct Illinois delegates for the Governor. On May 2 Dawes received a letter from Canton. "There is nothing in all of this long campaign so signal and significant as the triumph at Springfield," wrote McKinley. Then he added the words which made all the hard work seem worth while: "You have won exceptional honor. You had long ago won my heart."

After Illinois, the press conceded the nomination to McKinley.

"The walls of the anti-McKinley Jericho are knocked too flat by the blast of the Illinois trumpet to be rebuilt," commented the New York *Evening Post.* "Quay and Platt and Manley make a dismal pretense at continued cheerfulness, but they see the fatal drift away from them, and know it cannot be checked." The bosses did not maintain the pretense very long, however, for they were soon issuing statements about McKinley's unfitness. At least Platt was. The Governor, he said, was not an astute leader; he was "simply a clever gentleman, much too amiable and much too impressionable to be safely intrusted with great executive office." Quay took his defeat with better grace. He visited Canton in an effort to smooth things over as best he could. Yet McKinley's rout of the bosses, as New York publisher Whitelaw Reid pointed out, relieved him of any necessity "to offer them many premiums to reward them for not committing suicide." Quay was treated with kindness; it was as much as he could expect.

In the meantime hatemongers had gone to work on McKinley and his organization. The Hearst papers printed stories about the lavish expenditures of Hanna and his aides. A bottomless slush fund was supposed to have been used to buy the votes of delegates to the convention. Hanna did not dignify the Hearst attacks by answering, but they were doubtless exaggerated. Even more insidious were the activities of the American Protective Association. Thinking men would long since have given up the sort of charges that the association bandied about; they were tenuous in the extreme and ineffective as well. But the A.P.A. was not a thinking man's organization. On April 10 the chairman of its advisory board issued a statement that the records of all Republican candidates had been examined and that only McKinley was found wanting. He had presumably fired members of the A.P.A. from government jobs in Ohio in order to appoint Catholics. This charge was mild compared to what was whispered by A.P.A. men in their more frenetic moments. Yet the hate groups never made much headway. McKinley and Hanna wisely let them burn themselves out.

Silence may be the best response to slander, but it is not the best response to legitimate criticism. The most serious weakness in McKinley's candidacy was his reluctance to comment on the money question, rapidly becoming the one issue everybody wanted to talk about. The advance agent of prosperity had a clearer understanding of economics than had most of his fellow politicians. But for the moment it was the politics of tariff revision that interested him as he tried to make it the paramount issue of '96. He viewed free silver in political terms too, and McKinley the practical politician believed that in ambiguity on the money question there was strength. In his preliminary campaign he saw no need to antagonize western delegates by coming out for gold or eastern delegates by coming out for silver. "McKinley isn't a gold-bug, McKinley isn't a silver-bug," Thomas B. Reed is supposed to have said, "McKinley's a straddle-bug."

When queried, the Governor was inclined to use the old dodge that his record spoke for itself. What did the record say? As a member of the House of Representatives he had voted for the Bland free coinage bill in 1877. He had also voted for the compromise Bland-Allison bill, and when President Hayes vetoed it, he voted to override the President's veto. As chairman of the resolutions committee of the Republican National Convention of 1888, McKinley had reported a platform which declared that "the Republican party is in favor of the use of both gold and silver as money." The plank went on to condemn the Cleveland administration for recommending repeal of the Bland-Allison Act. In 1890, when he was chairman of the House Ways and Means Committee, McKinley had urged the passage of the Sherman Silver Purchase Act. "We cannot have free coinage now, except in the manner provided in the bill," he had said then. "To defeat this bill means to defeat all silver legislation and to leave us with two millions a month only, when by passing this bill we would have four and a half millions a month of Treasury notes as good as gold."

The record was not one that was likely to bring cheers from financial circles. But then the record of the Republican party as a whole was hardly a model of consistency. Over the years the GOP had developed a reasonably well-defined position on the tariff. The silver question was a different case entirely. Whatever the party had said on that issue had been justified primarily on grounds of political expediency. If McKinley's attitude seemed vague, then, it was no more so than that of his party.

One thing was certain. While the Governor might evade the issue, at least until after his nomination, he would choose for gold if he had to make a choice. To calm the sound money men Senator Sherman wrote a letter in McKinley's behalf. The candidate, said Sherman, "is opposed to the free coinage of silver upon the present ratio, and is in favor of the maintenance of all forms of money at par with gold." But to the last McKinley held to the vain hope that a compromise on bimetallism could be worked out and that he would be free to campaign on the tariff.

Despite criticism, McKinley's preliminary canvass had been so successful that his organization was in almost complete control of the St. Louis convention. All the leading McKinley men—Hanna, Dawes, Joe Smith, Will Osborne—were on the scene a week before the delegates were scheduled to convene. With a telegraphic system between St. Louis and Canton and a private telephone connecting Hanna's headquarters with the Governor's home, no important step was taken at the convention without McKinley's approval. He made all the major decisions. So firmly did he hold the reins that the conclave promised to become one of the dullest in party history.

The controversy over gold and the money question, however, redeemed the convention from utter tedium. While McKinley had not spoken out publicly on the money plank, he had given it considerable thought, and he had asked for advice from associates. He roughed out a plank calling for sound money and opposing free coinage of silver at 16 to 1. There was no mention of gold in his original draft. What he had written he then sent around as a memorandum to several prominent men for comments. The result was a formula which Hanna turned over to a privy council of McKinley men in St. Louis That small group of perhaps a dozen or so labored to produce a plank which could be presented to the convention. The formula they were given was much like McKinley's rough draft; it opposed free silver and emphasized "the plain duty of the United States to maintain our present standard."

After lengthy discussion and a round of consultation the group decided to recommend that the platform come out openly for the preservation of the "existing gold standard." There was no difference between standing for the maintenance of the present standard and standing for the preservation of the existing gold standard. That so much importance was attached to the word "gold" suggests that McKinley and his followers were still thinking in political rather than economic terms. The decision to insert the controversial word involved some nice political calculations. The West, reasoned McKinley and Hanna, could not be won by straddling, in fact could not be won by anything less than free silver. The West must therefore be sacrificed in order to hold the East. As for the vital North Central States, Hanna the industrialist and McKinley the champion of protection gambled that urban-industrial elements would go heavily Republican and would outvote any agrarians who might be driven into other parties.

With the gold plank worked out, the McKinley organization anticipated few difficulties in the convention. Delegates arriving in time for the opening ceremonies on June 16 found St. Louis already draped in red, white, and blue bunting and plastered with McKinley posters. They cheered dutifully when temporary chairman Charles W. Fairbanks told them that the American people were looking hopefully and confidently to the Republican party. "Three years of Democratic administration," he said, "have been three years of panic, of wasted energy, of anxiety and loss to the American people, without parallel in our history." He pointed with pride to the Republican record in commerce and foreign affairs. But the great questions for debate, he said, were "Free Trade and Free Silver against a Protective Tariff and Sound Money."

What drama there was in the GOP proceedings in St. Louis came on June 18, the third day of the convention. It was then that Senator-elect Foraker, Chairman of the Resolutions Committee, presented the platform. That document called for a revision of the tariff according to Republican, that is to say protectionist, principles. It favored control of the Hawaiian Islands by the United States and the construction of a canal in Nicaragua. Sympathy was extended to the people of Cuba in their struggle against tyranny. Among the other planks were demands for generous pensions, a larger navy, exclusion of illiterate immigrants, a national board of arbitration to settle labor disputes, and statehood for the remaining territories at the earliest possible date.

This of course was not all. If it had been, peace and harmony would have reigned. "We are unalterably opposed to every measure calculated to debase our currency or impair the credit of our country," read Foraker as he came to the section of the platform most delegates considered of prime importance. "We are therefore opposed to the free coinage of silver, except by international agreement with the leading nations of the earth. . . ." At this point he was interrupted by a demonstration that lasted for several minutes. With order restored he continued, "which agreement we pledge ourselves to promote, and until such agreement can be obtained the existing gold standard must be maintained." There it was. The word was out and the political realignment that had been developing for several years became as certain as anything can be in politics.

The convention welcomed the declaration for gold with such enthusiasm that few observers noted the promise to work for bimetallism through international agreement. In any event, efforts to secure such an agreement had failed in the past, and the pledge offered silver men little hope. In one of the most futile maneuvers in the annals of the GOP Senator Henry Moore Teller of Colorado read a minority report in behalf of the silverites. No one in the convention hall knew better than he did how futile it was. Nevertheless he insisted, "I cannot before my country and my God, agree to the provision that shall put upon this country a gold standard, and I will not." Despite Teller's tears, the vote crushed his substitute free silver plank, 812½ to 110½. The platform as reported out by the committee was immediately adopted viva voce.

The silver men now took their leave of the convention. They had prepared a statement which Utah's dapper young Senator, Frank Cannon, read to unappreciative delegates. It described the adoption of the gold plank as "the greatest wrong ever willfully attempted within the Republican party, once the redeemer of the people, but now about to become their oppressor unless Providentially restrained." Hisses and catcalls punctuated the reading of such sentences. William Allen White, sitting near Mark Hanna at the time, recalled later that "a steel sneer wired its ways across his face" as he listened to Cannon. When the speaker used the expression "the parting of the ways," Hanna was one of the first to shout, "Good-bye!" Then the band played "Columbia" as Teller led twenty-two silverites down the aisle and out the door.

When the convention calmed down, the chairman, Senator Thurston of Nebraska, commented dryly, "Gentlemen of the Convention: There seems [*sic*] to be enough delegates left to transact the business of the Convention." The remaining business had in effect already been transacted. All the delegates had to do was nominate William McKinley and his running mate; then they could go home. Without interruption the convention proceeded to the naming of candidates for the nomination. Although McKinley's victory was assured, the bosses refused to concede. To what was for them a bitter end, they continued to act as though one of the favorite sons had a chance. Allison was the first to be named, and speeches for Reed, Morton, McKinley, and Quay followed in that order. Foraker, well practiced by now in the art of nominating McKinley, had never been more eloquent, and his remarks were enthusiastically received. When he mentioned the Governor's name, he was interrupted by a twenty-five minute demonstration. At last permitted to continue, he said, "You seem to have heard the name of my candidate before. And so you have. He is known to all the world."

It was over quickly. Alabama cast 19 votes for McKinley, 2 for Reed, and 1 for Morton. Arkansas gave all of its 16 votes to McKinley, and California contributed its 18. So it went. The Major, with several close friends, sat in his study in Canton quietly marking his tally sheet as the votes came in. The totals mounted rapidly, and

Ohio's 46 votes gave McKinley the nomination. That his own state should put him over the top was a good omen, one that was contemplated with satisfaction as the little Ohio town went wild with joy. While Canton celebrated, the delegates dutifully named McKinley's choice, New Jersey lawyer-businessman Garret A. Hobart, for Vice President.

In the waning hours of the convention Mark Hanna rose to pronounce his benediction on the proceedings. Chauncey Depew had just referred to the importance of the American people in the campaign. Hanna, in his thin, high-pitched voice, commented briefly on the same theme: "I am glad that there was one member of this convention who has the intelligence at this late hour to ascertain how this nomination was made. By the people." There was something in what Hanna said; McKinley had shown that he commanded widespread and enthusiastic support, and his popularity with voters helped to account for his success.

Nevertheless Hanna had been superb as a tactician at St. Louis. The way in which he had kept his intentions from the anti-McKinley faction until the right moment for making concessions was an object lesson in how to win by letting one's opponent think he has accomplished something. Small wonder that Platt and others who had had nothing to do with the wording of the gold plank later claimed credit for it. Actually everything had gone according to the script McKinley and Hanna had written. There was, to be sure, a lack of spontaneity in the proceedings. "The applause is hollow; the enthusiasm dreary and the delegates sit like hogs in a car and know nothing about anything," reported William Allen White. Probably McKinley and Hanna would never rival Gilbert and Sullivan in showmanship, but they did achieve most of their objectives. There is something to be said for that.

VI

SILVER AND THE DEMOCRATS

IN THE EARLY MONTHS OF 1896 THE ATTENTION OF REpublicans throughout the country centered on William McKinley's campaign for the GOP nomination. Whether party members supported the Major or opposed him, they did not doubt that the future turned upon his success or failure. Up until the eve of the St. Louis convention, intraparty battles were essentially personality conflicts. Republicans concerned themselves primarily with candidates rather than with issues. The reasons for such concern were many, but they came down to the fact that party leaders agreed on essential issues. As has been noted, only silver was potentially divisive, and McKinley conducted his preconvention campaign in such a way as to postpone an open break on that question.

When the convention met at last, it was obvious to everyone that the struggle for the nomination was already over. The adoption of a platform thus became the chief order of business. Like it or not, Republicans would have to face the silver issue; postponement was no longer possible. McKinley finally came out for gold, and the convention cheerfully accepted his wording of the money plank. When the delegates so readily approved this shrewdly calculated move of their predestined candidate, they certainly did not make the most unexpected decision in Republican party history. But it was an important decision nevertheless. It put to rest the only doubts anyone had about the position of the GOP in 1896.

Within the Democratic party, meanwhile, developments took an entirely different course. Cleveland's efforts to overcome the depression of the nineties were based in large part upon a doctrinaire belief in the gold standard. Convinced of the soundness of his monetary theory, he placed party unity in jeopardy in order to act upon it. Unfortunately, nothing worked out as the President had hoped. When his program failed to bring recovery, both the program and the theory on which it was based were vigorously attacked. His fellow Democrats from the West and South led the attack, and Republicans watched in high glee as internecine strife threatened the Democracy with disruption for the second time in fifty years.

Cleveland was of a mind to let the party crack up rather than to yield to silver inflationists. Silver men felt just as strongly that the money question was of greater importance than party affiliation, and they too were prepared to sacrifice party for principle if it came to that. But many of them did not think it would come to that. For the time being at least silver Democrats concentrated their energies on building up a following for silver. Perhaps if the work of evangelization went well, they could take over the party organization from Cleveland and his Bourbon cohorts.

The very nature of the struggle within the Democratic party made the money question paramount. While Republicans were thinking about candidates, Democrats were thinking about silver. While William McKinley slowly and surely won Republican delegations to his cause, silver men won Democratic delegations to theirs. The St. Louis convention of the GOP was dominated by McKinley; the Chicago convention of the Democracy was dominated by silver. Aside from McKinley's nomination, which was assured by his preliminary campaign, the most important action taken by the Republicans at St. Louis was the adoption of the gold plank. Aside from the endorsement of silver, almost as much a certainty as McKinley's nomination, the most important action taken by the Democrats at Chicago was the nomination of William Jennings Bryan for President.

If the Democratic gathering seemed much more exciting and dramatic than the Republican conclave, it was in part because of the remarkable success of the young orator from the Plains. But orators must have something to discuss. They are best able to produce electrifying results when they are orating on issues about which men feel deeply. Voice, technique, rhetoric—all these are important, but not so important as a cause. Bryan and the silver Democrats battled for a cause at Chicago, and the convention was exciting and dramatic because it climaxed a long campaign to win the party for silver.

The work of setting up an organization through which silver forces could exert their influence had been started as early as 1889. In that year the St. Louis Mining Stock Exchange, following a suggestion of the mining editor of the *Post-Dispatch,* called for a meeting of silver men to develop a program for the consideration of Congress. When it met late in November, the conference was attended by many who were to be influential in the silver crusade of the nineties. General Adoniram J. Warner, a Union Army veteran and successful dealer in railroad coal and iron, came from his home in Marietta, Ohio. His reputation as an advocate of silver and his commanding presence (a six footer, he looked like a large size General Grant) impressed the delegates. He was chosen permanent chairman of the convention and chairman of the standing National Executive Committee appointed to carry on the work for silver.

Heading the list of speakers at St. Louis were two men who had spent several years in the mining fields of the West before entering politics. One was Richard Parks Bland, Missouri's perennial advocate of free silver in the House of Representatives and co-author of the Bland-Allison Act. The other was Nevada Senator William M. Stewart, an expert on mining law whose fat fees from mining companies provided him with considerable wealth and a personal stake in the silver movement. But neither Bland nor Stewart was so foolish as to speak solely from the point of view of western mining interests. Along with other speakers they rang the changes on their favorite theme: that the whole country was suffering at the hands of international gold conspirators. From the very beginning of silver agitation free coinage was regarded as a means of uniting the common people against the bondholding and moneyed classes.

Shortly after the St. Louis meeting General Warner went to Washington, where he set up headquarters for a silver lobby subsequently named the American Bimetallic League. But the first real efforts to develop a total organization of silver forces coincided with the Panic of 1893. Just before Cleveland's second inauguration silver leaders met in Washington and resolved to invite every labor and industrial group in the country to send delegates to future meetings of the American Bimetallic League.

Over eight hundred silverites attended the next League sessions held in Chicago on the first two days of August, 1893. Cleveland had called upon Congress to meet the week following; Bourbon leaders and their allies were planning to repeal the Sherman Silver Purchase Act. Tension in Chicago ran high as delegates prepared to meet the crisis. William Jennings Bryan sat with the resolutions committee where for the first time he met its chairman, Ignatius Donnelly. The report of the committee, enthusiastically adopted by the conference, asserted that "the unparalleled calamities which now afflict the American people" were not the result of the Sherman Act but of manipulations which demonetized silver in 1873. It declared that "the only remedy for our metallic financial trouble is to open the mints of the Nation to gold and silver on equal terms at the old ratio of sixteen of silver to one of gold."

The hard money press of course took a dim view of the resolutions adopted in Chicago. "It is, upon the whole, well that the mixed assortment of demagogues and maniacs was brought together under circumstances that admitted of a good view by the public of its component parts," remarked the Brooklyn *Citizen* in its report of the conference. "The man who cannot now see that they are little more than a pack of brainless dupes and impudent humbugs blended, ought to turn his attention to something less complicated than the money question." Such name calling had little effect on League leaders, however, as they fashioned instruments for more effective coordination.

The task of organization was not an easy one. If there was general agreement on basic objectives, there were differences of opinion on the relationship between the American Bimetallic League and established political parties. Some delegates favored a plan by which all parties would be represented on committees. Others wished to form a new party. Still others thought that parties should be ignored. Populists were particularly active in 1893. Proud of their recent achievements and optimistically looking forward to future successes, they wanted others to accept their leadership. The nonpartisan character of the League was maintained, but how long it could continue to remain nonpartisan was a nice question.

Western and southern agrarians demanded and received special recognition. Coming from sections where silver sentiment was strongest, they placed men in key positions. H. E. Taubeneck, chairman of the Populist party, became a member of the League's executive committee. Ignatius Donnelly was appointed to a subcommittee charged with publicizing silver. So was Reuben F. Kolb, a prominent Populist from Alabama. It was a dangerous game these men were playing. They doubtless had visions of establishing Populist control over the silver movement. If so, they did not fully reckon with the possibility that influence could be exerted in the opposite direction. The nose of the silver camel was already beginning to appear under the Populist tent.

Whatever course Populists might take, the Chicago conference spurred silverites on to new endeavor. The third national silver convention of 1893 met in St. Louis in October, and it produced the usual declaration for free coinage. After that, announcements of conferences and conventions came thick and fast as state organizations were established and silver clubs formed. Everybody was beginning to talk about silver and numbers of citizens were already doing something about it. The summer of 1894, with congressional elections in the offing, was a strenuous one for leaders of the movement. Silver remained a sectional rather than a party issue, yet the demand for speakers on the subject reached a new high. The best of the silver orators—men such as Senator John Warwick Daniel, the "Lame Lion" of Virginia, and Republican Senator John P. Jones of Nevada, whose address in the Senate opposing repeal of the Sherman Act had been hailed as a classic—were overwhelmed with invitations to speak.

No one gave more freely of his time and talent than did William Jennings Bryan. He spoke often, but two dates were of particular importance. On June 21 he attended a convention of Nebraska's silver Democrats which had been called to meet in Omaha. If any doubt had existed that Bryan was the commander of silver forces in his home state, it was soon dispelled after his Omaha speech. Some Nebraskans had favored a general declaration for bimetallism, but the convention adopted Bryan's bolder demand for immediate free coinage at 16 to 1. Delegates then proceeded to set up a silver organization which reached into every county and many precincts and which stood ready to follow Bryan wherever he might lead.

The young Congressman's second important speaking engagement during the summer of 1894 was in Washington where the American Bimetallic League held a conference on August 16 and 17. Bryan appeared on the program along with Senator Jones and Congressman Bland, a clear indication that he enjoyed national stature. The conference published a report pointing out that repeal of the Sherman Act had failed to bring recovery and that passage of the Wilson-Gorman Act had disposed of the tariff issue. The way had therefore been prepared for silver, and the report predicted that it would become the paramount issue in future campaigns.

As silver men began to think about readying themselves for the next presidential election, General Warner issued a call to all friends of bimetallism to meet in St. Louis in November. The conference coincided with a meeting of the Trans-Mississippi Commercial Congress, and Bryan took an active part in both conventions. He became chairman of the resolutions committee of the Congress, and although it was not really a silver organization, he managed to secure the passage of resolutions favoring free coinage. By this time the attractiveness of silver to large numbers of men in all parties was so evident that Warner and others were beginning to consider forming an independent silver party.

The step was not taken at St. Louis, however, for no one wished to establish a new party if it would result in controversy rather than solidarity. Yet the work of education was going well, and it seemed to many that the time for political effort had arrived. Finally an elite group of the American Bimetallic League met in Washington from February 22 to March 5, 1895, for a long, serious discussion of the problem. Most of the big names of the silver movement took part. Warner was there, of course. So were Bryan, Bland, Teller, Stewart, and Jones. After some deliberation, the group decided to announce the formation of the American Bimetallic party. Its supporters defended the action on grounds that "no course seems possible but to subordinate for the time being other questions and come together in a new organization to fight the great battle of 1896 on the one great issue on which the prosperity and happiness of the people so largely depend."

Although it was still too early to select a candidate, the group in Washington discussed various possibilities. Bryan's name was brought up, as were names of the other men prominent in the silver movement. Two colorful personalities from Pennsylvania enjoyed support. One was Don Cameron who was as thoroughgoing a Republican as had been his father, Lincoln's Secretary of War, or his wife's uncle, John Sherman. Henry Adams, who knew Cameron well, described him as "a practical politician, whom all reformers, including the Adamses, had abused for a lifetime for subservience to moneyed interests and political jobbery." Yet paradoxically instead of going along with the banks and corporations which had boosted him to power, Cameron stood obstinately as a champion of silver. The other Pennsylvanian was Joseph C. Sibley, a producer of special oils, an advocate and practitioner of scientific farming and stock breeding, and a dabbler in causes. In 1892 he had run for Congress in a normally Republican district; and with the support of Democrats, Populists, and Prohibitionists he had won.

Sibley was the man tapped by the Washington conference as the most available candidate at the time. Together with General Warner he toured the country during 1895, campaigning for silver and incidentally for himself. Few people really took the Sibley candidacy seriously, but none of the silverites objected to his discussing the issue. Many of them doubtless felt as did Bryan that it was still too early in the game to make commitments. The Nebraskan, now editor of the Omaha *World Herald,* refused to be trapped. Although he had been active in the Washington conference, he let it be known that he could not in good conscience leave the Democratic party unless the party repudiated silver at its national convention in 1896.

During 1895 and the first part of 1896 Bryan was frequently on the road. He addressed convention after convention, and when he was not speaking on silver he was writing editorials about it. If voters were not well informed on issues in the coming election, it would be through no fault of his. And it would not be his fault either if the Democracy did, in fact, repudiate silver. In mid-June, 1895, Bryan shared the spotlight with Governor John Peter Altgeld when Illinois Democrats met at Springfield. Both men were gratified by the enthusiasm of the delegates and the passage of a free-coinage resolution. Equally encouraging was similar action taken by Democrats in Texas, Mississippi, and Missouri.

From Springfield Bryan moved on to Memphis, where silver Democrats met on June 18. This conference was a response to meetings of Bourbon Democrats which had been held in the same city in May. Bryan was again one of the principal speakers, and once more he emphasized his loyalty to the Democracy if the Democracy would pledge its loyalty to silver. All indications pointed toward a powerful silver movement within the party as arrangements were made for a conference of free-silver Democrats to meet in Washington on August 14 and 15. It was not a large conference—only about eighty delegates attended—but it was an important one, for some of the foremost Democrats in the country shared in its proceedings.

Among those most active were Senators James K. Jones of Arkansas, Isham G. Harris of Tennessee, Thomas J. Jarvis of North Carolina, Wilkinson Call of Florida, and John W. Daniel of Virginia. These men had strikingly similar backgrounds. All had been advocates of states' rights before the Civil War, and all of them were veterans of the Confederate Army. They upheld a southern political tradition that reached backward through Calhoun to Jefferson. The southern senators were joined in their labors now by state officials such as Missouri's moderate Governor, William J. Stone, and the Secretary of State of Illinois, W. H. Hinrichsen. Both Stone and Hinrichsen were close friends of Bryan, but Bryan himself did not attend the conference.

The intentions of the silver Democrats could be read into their announcement that "the Democratic party is the traditional friend and champion of bimetallism." Clearly they hoped to do what Populist leaders had tried to do at the Chicago silver convention of 1893: win control of the silver movement. To that end they appointed an executive committee with Senators Harris and Jones, Senator David Turpie of Indiana, Governor Stone, and W. H. Hinrichsen as members. At the same time a larger body, a national committee made up of one member from each state and territory, was organized. Each committeeman pledged himself to establish Democratic silver clubs in every county and precinct in his state.

The small size of the Washington conference which created the Democratic silver organization led some newspapers to speculate that silver agitation would soon pass. The Baltimore *Sun* found "cheering evidence everywhere that the silver hallucination is fast losing its hold upon the popular mind," and the Philadelphia *Times* discussed the imminent disappearance of the "silver craze." But the Atlanta *Constitution* took a different position. "What are the signs of its moribund condition?" demanded the *Constitution*. "An immense mass meeting at Memphis, a convention of the people of the State of Georgia, a convention of the people of Missouri, a unanimous declaration on the part of the people of Mississippi, a meeting of the most prominent Democratic workers in Washington—and all in favor of the free, unlimited, and independent coinage of silver at the ratio of 16 to 1."

The silver crusade was not by any means slowing down, but toward the end of 1895 signs of disunity began to appear. Middle-of-the-road Populists, as the radical faction of the party styled itself, insisted that free silver was only one reform among many which were essential for prosperity. Others, such as James B. Weaver and Marion Butler, argued that Populists could best win votes by emphasizing silver. Silver Republicans from the West hesitated to leave their party. Senator Stewart did join the Populists, but Senator Teller stayed with the GOP until that bitter moment when he walked out of the St. Louis convention. Silver Democrats had to face the possibility of continued Bourbon control of their party, but they hoped to win over all other dissident elements by making it the party of silver. The hitherto nonpartisan American Bimetallic League had founded an independent silver party, and no one knew but what it might become the party of the future. There were, in addition, newly formed silver groups such as the National Bimetallic Union which might eventually emerge as rivals of older organizations. Hearts were full of passion for silver, but silver leagues, clubs, unions, and factions had so proliferated that jealousies and hatreds were perhaps unavoidable.

In the meantime, propaganda on the money question flooded the country. Silverites doubtless had the better of it in the field of polemical literature. Certainly gold men never produced anything quite so effective as William H. Harvey's series of tracts which featured a precocious adolescent named Coin. Thousands of voters were introduced to the "smooth little financier" in 1894 when *Coin's Financial School* appeared. The book was ostensibly an account of lectures given by Coin at the Chicago Art Institute, and it included debates he was supposed to have had with the most distinguished opponents of silver. In all his encounters with bankers and businessmen, the boy wizard forced his opponents to concede the errors of their ways.

One of his many triumphs, as described by Harvey, came in an encounter with Lyman Gage, president of the First National Bank of Chicago. "How can you have, at any fixed ratio, the same commercial value on two separate metals, that are from time to time varying in the quantity of each produced?" Gage asked. Coin replied to this "stock fallacy" of the gold monometallists by drawing on the blackboard two reservoirs filled with water and connected by a pipe. "Now, the water in one of these reservoirs represents silver and the other gold," said the little economist. "The connecting pipe [the law of free coinage] makes them virtually one metal and either answers the requirement of the government for money. So long as that connecting pipe remains, the water in the two reservoirs will remain even—the same height. Do away with the connecting pipe and the feed pipes . . . will soon destroy the equilibrium, as their quantities vary from time to time." Gage and his friends could detect here no errors of reasoning. Instead of scoffing at Coin, they were "compelled to give assent to his plain and unanswerable views."

Harvey wrote so plausibly that his books became immediate best sellers, and gold men rushed to attack Coin's arguments. In 1895 they came out with such titles as *Coin's Financial Fraud; Bullion vs. Coin; Cash vs. Coin; A Freak in Finance, or the Boy Teacher Taught; Farmer Hayseed in Town, or The Closing Days of Coin's Financial School; Mistakes of Coin; Coin's Financial Fool, or The Artful Dodger Exposed;* and *Base "Coin" Exposed, Being the Arrest, Exposure and Confession of W. H. H. Money, and the Dismissal of the So-Called "Coin's Financial School" by Silas Honest Money.* But abuse could not wither nor calumny stale the infinite variety of Coin's quick wit and dialectical skill. Silver men took him to their hearts. There were other silver panegyrists, of course. Like Harvey, Ignatius Donnelly employed dialogue in writing *The American People's Money,* a conversation between a banker and a farmer who chanced to be traveling companions on a train from Chicago to the

Pacific Coast. Yet not even Donnelly could match the popularity of the little school teacher.

Discussion of the money question sometimes ran toward extremism and sophistry on both sides. Many silverites harped on the theme of conspiracy and double-dealing. One Nebraska farmer wrote Bryan that the so-called sound money adherents "would if possible dispossess *Christ* of his throne and sell out the chances of Heaven for Government Gold bearing bonds." In the vast mass of contemporary silver literature one finds an occasional anti-Semitic piece such as Ebenezer Wakeley's *The Gentile Ass and the Judean Monetary Establishment*, but works of that kind were rare. When anti-foreign prejudice found expression, it was almost invariably directed against British bankers. Thus in a work entitled *Shylock*, Gordon Clark had as much to say about English greed and the iniquities of the Bank of England as he did about "Ricardo's hebraic gold-bugs."

Whether anti-Semitic or Anglophobic, the contentions of such extremists obviously missed the point. Champions of the gold standard were equally wide of the mark when they characterized all proponents of silver as cranks and misfits. "Who are your followers, Harvey?" demanded Roswell Horr, former Congressman and editor of the New York *Tribune*, when the two men met in debate. "Is it that the philosophers and sages of the civilized world are all ignoramuses and that we can get no wisdom except we look for it in this crowd of populists—I cannot use the proper words that would express my feelings. . . ." The proper words, some gold men seem to have felt, were those they used so often: "rag-tag, bob-tail," "rapscallion element," "witness dupes," "ignorant and inferior men."

Fortunately, however, discussion of the money question sometimes—in fact, often—avoided such extremes. In 1896 when Professor J. Lawrence Laughlin of the University of Chicago published the the second edition of his *History of Bimetallism*, one of the soundest of the sound money books, he did not castigate the proponents of silver. And when Bryan in the same year met Editor Victor Rosewater of the *Omaha Bee* in public debate, he was reasonableness itself. Bryan argued that "a dollar which rises in purchasing power benefits the creditor and injures the debtor." But on the other hand he admitted that "a dollar which falls in value hurts the creditor and helps the debtor and stimulates speculation." He did not want either one. "If I could have the dollar which I desire, I would have one which would neither rise nor fall," said Bryan. "But we are confronted by a proposition; we are met by a condition. We must endure the gold standard, with an appreciating dollar, or we must return to bimetallism and bear whatever temporary injury that brings in order to reach a more stable basis." With Bryan's basic objectives few men would disagree, and the silver discussion at its best was like most great debates in American politics. It centered on means rather than ends.

Yet many Americans were little interested in arguments except insofar as those arguments could be used to buttress positions they had already taken. "Free silver with me is not a theory at all, it is a conviction," commented an Iowan. "I believe in it." So did thousands of men in the West and South, and the political problem which faced silver leaders at the opening of the year 1896 was not so much a problem of persuading voters to accept their views as it was a problem of providing unity and control for the forces of silver. The time had come for new organizational efforts.

The most important victory for consolidation yet achieved occurred on January 22 and 23, 1896. It was then that a conference encompassing the most vigorous of the national silver associations, particularly the American Bimetallic League, the National Bimetallic Union, and the National Executive Silver Committee, met in Washington. The conference issued the usual address to the American people in which it reiterated the usual arguments for free silver. But the address also appealed to citizens "to leave in abeyance for the moment all other questions, however important and even momentous they may appear, to sunder, if need be, all former party ties and affiliations, and unite in one supreme effort to free themselves and their children from the domination of the money power. . . ." The old organizations were disbanded, and provisions were made for two new ones to take their place. One, a nonpolitical educational agency, was to be known as the American Bimetallic Union; the other, a political party, was somewhat awkwardly styled the American Silver Organization, and most people referred to it simply as the Silver party.

General Warner, still in the front ranks of the silver movement, became chairman of the American Bimetallic Union. The conference agreed that offices of the agency should be set up in Washington, Chicago, and San Francisco and that it should take over publication of the *National Bimetallist,* an organ of the old National Bimetallic Union. As for the Silver party, the conference decided that it should hold its national nominating convention in St. Louis on July 22, 1896. Silver leaders chose the date after consultation with the national committee of the Populist party, and the Populists agreed to hold their convention at the same time and place.

No effort was spared in preparing for a united silver action in the election of 1896. To be sure, large numbers of silver men had maintained relationships with the Republican and Democratic parties. But leaders of the Populist party confidently expected silver Republicans and Democrats to bolt sometime during the year, perhaps after national conventions had been held. This was the rationale for holding the Populist convention so late. In January the executive committee still believed that both of the old parties would adopt gold planks. When that occurred, and the old parties had been shattered, Populists would be ready to pick up the pieces.

The reasoning of the simon-pure silverites who convened in Washington was not precisely the same as that of the Populists, though it was no less opportunistic. Not so certain of a split in the Democratic party, they fondly hoped that both Democrats and Populists would be persuaded to make the silver issue paramount. If traditional Democratic doctrines on the tariff and other matters were held in abeyance, and if Populists did not insist on their reforms in land and transportation, silver men foresaw great possibilities in silver fusion all along the line. Of course, even if it turned out that the Democrats did follow Grover Cleveland and his gold-bug friends, the cause of fusion would not necessarily suffer. Union of silver Republicans, silver Democrats, and Populists could still be effected under the auspices of the American Silver Organization.

The decade of the nineties did not favor plungers, and Populists acted the part of plungers in betting that both Republicans and Democrats would come out for gold. The greater insight—or if one prefers, the greater luck—of the single-minded silver men became apparent during the spring of 1896 as state Democratic organizations selected delegates to the party's national convention in Chicago. Oregon Democrats, the first to convene, named a silver delegation on April 9. The party conventions in Missouri, Colorado, and Washington followed Oregon's lead on April 15 when they instructed their men to vote for silver. Week after week delegations were announced. As leaders of the silver movement had guessed, the states of the West and South overwhelmingly supported silver. By convention time delegations pledged to free coinage were in a top-heavy majority; and when a few contesting gold delegates had been eliminated, the silver men would have the two-thirds vote necessary to nominate the candidate of their choice.

The success of the silverites resulted from vigorous and effective campaigning by the Bimetallic Democratic National Committee. That committee had established reliable organizations in each of the states west of the Alleghenies and south of Maryland, and its thoroughness had paid off. The Bourbon Democrats had done little to develop any sort of organization to combat their silver rivals. Only when it became clear that they had lost the West and South did they bestir themselves in the Middle West. Even then, they did not have the stomach to make much of a campaign of it. Cleveland's friend and former Postmaster General, Don Dickinson, wrote the President from Michigan that he was disinclined to take a gold delegation to the Chicago convention. His feeling that Republicans were headed toward a landslide victory in November conditioned his behavior. "It seems to me that if a bad defeat must come anyway," he wrote, "it had better be with a crank platform, as well as with a candidate who would not carry a Northern state and probably not half the South."

Other administration men doubtless felt as did Dickinson. Cleveland nevertheless urged his followers to do what they could, and in the upper Middle West, at least, they enjoyed some success. The Michigan convention under Dickinson's leadership approved Cleveland's stand on the money question. With relatively little difficulty William Freeman Vilas kept Wisconsin Democrats true to the President. Minnesota also came out for gold, but the Bourbon leader there, Michael Doran, thought the cause so hopeless that he washed his hands of the whole business and escaped to Europe. Outside of New York, Pennsylvania, New Jersey, and the New England states these were the only significant victories for Cleveland in the preconvention campaign.

With reports of state victories coming in with gratifying regularity, silver Democrats gave increasing attention to possible candidates. During that spring of 1896 the front-runner and clearly the man to beat for the nomination was Richard Parks Bland. The old war horse of the free-silver movement had the respect of all who favored a free-coinage law, and he also had assistance from the most influential men in the silver wing of the Democratic party. The Governor of his own state, William J. Stone, worked hard for him. Senator James K. Jones favored his nomination. Senator Tillman promised him the votes of the South Carolina delegation. Most of the members of the Bimetallic Democratic National Committee looked upon him with kindly eyes. But no doubt his strongest supporter was Governor Altgeld, the man later featured in Republican campaign literature as the dictator of the Chicago convention, and himself a good possibility for the nomination were it not for his foreign birth.

Yet the Democratic silver organization did not formally espouse the candidacy of any one leader, and other hopefuls were free to campaign for a following. Second only to Bland among those mentioned prior to the convention was Horace Boies, former Governor of Iowa. The soul of discretion, Boies avoided a vigorous fight for the nomination. As a moderate he had for a long time maintained that he was for bimetallism without mentioning any ratio; only recently had he come out for 16 to 1. For one regarded by many Democrats as too much of a pussyfooter, Boies had made some courageous decisions during his political career. A Republican, he had left his party in 1889 when it supported prohibition in Iowa. He had joined the Democrats and, campaigning on the prohibition question, had been elected Governor. Handsome and erect, he had been a candidate for the presidential nomination in 1892; now he appealed to the compromise-minded in 1896.

In addition to Bland and Boies there were lesser candidates in abundance. Among the conservatives and moderates who received consideration early in the preconvention campaign were a spate of former governors: Pattison of Pennsylvania, Russell of Massachusetts, Campbell of Ohio, and Matthews of Indiana. From Illinois came two politicians of temperate disposition who might become contenders should the platform straddle on the money question. They were Vice President Adlai Stevenson and Congressman William Ralls Morrison. Another moderate was John R. McLean, editor of the Cincinnati *Enquirer.* Senator Joseph C. S. Blackburn was immensely popular in his home state, Kentucky. The name of Secretary of the Treasury John G. Carlisle was also brought up, but his nomination would have been taken as a cruel joke.

Actually, as silver men gained control of the convention, it became clear that they would nominate one of their own. The most important though not necessarily the most likely possibilities were Benjamin F. Tillman, John W. Daniel, James K. Jones, and William Jennings Bryan. After the silver Republican bolt, Populists and others exerted pressure on Democrats to name Senator Teller. They argued that only he could unite the forces of silver without causing jealousy and dissension. Silver Democrats, notwithstanding their respect for Teller, rejected such pleas. Bryan expressed their feelings when he said "that we had won our fight in the Democratic party while the Republicans had lost their fight in the Republican party, and that it was easier to bring the disappointed Republicans over to the Democratic party than to carry the victorious Democrats over to the Republican party."

With the advantage of historical perspective it is easy to see that of all possible choices in or out of the Democratic party William Jennings Bryan had the best chance for the nomination. No one had been more active in the silver movement; yet no one had more deftly avoided tying himself to any particular organization. He had worked with Populists, the American Bimetallic Union, the Silver party, the Bimetallic Democratic National Committee, and several state silver organizations. He had made important friends in every association without raising honest doubts about his allegiance to the Democratic party. He had, of course, intimated that he would leave the party if it declared for gold, but given the composition of the Chicago convention there was no possibility that it would do any such thing.

Bryan was a master politician who moved adroitly and skillfully as the time for the convention approached. The wonder is not that he was eventually nominated. The wonder is that his contemporaries were so slow to recognize his nomination as, in his phrase, "the logic of the situation." Nevertheless Bryan took pains to avoid publicity as an avowed candidate. He did not have the means to carry on a campaign like the one Governor McKinley was waging. His strategy was to keep his name before the public through his speeches and editorials and to make himself known to as many Democrats as he could contact. From state silver leaders he secured the names of delegates to the convention; to each of them he sent copies of his addresses along with the silver plank he had written for Nebraska Democrats in 1894. While the delegates would not be thinking of the Nebraskan as a candidate, they would at least know who he was and what he had done. Then if the proper opportunity presented itself, who could tell what might happen?

To only a few close friends did Bryan admit his ambitions during the early months of 1896. Some of them had, in fact, been urging him to run. Josephus Daniels, the Tarheel editor, was an early supporter, as was Dr. Charles M. Rosser, a Texan who later became one of Bryan's biographers. "Your friends here are enthusiastically for you for the nomination," wrote John Tomlinson from Alabama in May. He pledged the editorial assistance of the Birmingham *State Herald.*

Not all of Bryan's friends thought he had a chance, however. Among the doubters was Governor Altgeld, who wrote that he found "everywhere great admiration for you but an almost unanimous sentiment that you are not available for president this time." Yet John H. Atwood, a well-known Kansas Democrat, expressed succinctly the consensus of Bryan's intimates: "Boies is too new a convert; Bland is too old and not brilliant enough; Blackburn is too far south; you alone have every quality that goes to make up my ideal of a silver candidate; you are young, clean and brilliant; now don't get the big head because I have said these things but it is as near the truth as the average Kansas lawyer ever gets." After receiving such expressions of confidence, Bryan became less reticent in discussing his chances. He was busier than ever during May and June. Finally the hour of decision was at hand.

Toward the end of June the air in Chicago seemed electric with suspense as silverites and reformers of every shade and description began to arrive. Fringe groups and some from beyond the fringe were represented. There were Coxeyites and Debsites, Prohibitionists and Suffragists, Socialists and Bellamy nationalists, all of them hoping to get a hearing for their special causes. Leaders of the Bimetallic Democratic National Committee also appeared on the scene early. On Monday, June 29, more than a week before the opening session, James K. Jones and T. O. Towles set up Committee headquarters. There the leaders of the silver movement held their caucuses and made their plans. Bourbons controlled the Democratic National Committee, but everybody knew they were on their way out. Thus the headquarters of the silver Democrats became the real nerve center of the convention.

Taking no chances, the silver leaders appointed a committee of five to keep a wary eye on the National Committee and National

Chairman William F. Harrity, who ironically enough happened to be a Philadelphia lawyer. The three senators (Jones, Turpie, and Daniel) and two governors (Altgeld and Stone) who made up the watchdog committee fully expected gold bugs to attempt a coup that would thwart the will of the silver majority in the convention. They warned Harrity that they would stand for no trickery, and the Chairman promised fair play. Administration men attempted nothing underhanded—perhaps they were not that interested—but when they finally put in an appearance they did go through the motions of trying to halt the stampede to silver.

William C. Whitney, former Secretary of the Navy and close friend of the President, cancelled a trip to Europe to attend the convention and take charge of the gold forces. Highly regarded as a skilled manager and tactician, Whitney hoped to secure a compromise plank calling for bimetallism through international agreement. On the train which took him to Chicago he talked things over with other sound money men such as David B. Hill, George Harvey, Thomas F. Ryan, and Don Dickinson. Isolated from unruly crowds and with good food and drink at hand they persuaded themselves that their mission had some chance of success. But then they arrived in Chicago, and everywhere they turned they saw silver banners and silver badges. A sound money rally which Whitney had scheduled for the evening of Saturday, July 3, and which was supposed to arouse delegates to a high pitch of enthusiasm for gold, proved a woeful failure. The sound money effort fizzled out like a wet firecracker before the dawn of July 4.

On Sunday and Monday trainloads of delegates came pouring into the city to be greeted by silver demonstrations that perhaps equaled in pyrotechnics any celebration since 1776. "This is to be one of the most remarkable conventions in the history of American politics," prophesied Republican Victor Rosewater, who was there to report the proceedings for the Omaha *Bee*. Later he added that "its action is certain to determine the future of the party for perhaps a generation to come."

When they finally convened on Tuesday, July 7, delegates were immediately thrown into an uproar over the report on organization submitted by the National Committee. The Committee named David B. Hill as temporary chairman; silver men proposed John W. Daniel instead, and the battle of the standards within the Democracy was on. In this instance precedent was on the side of the gold faction, for the National Committee customarily selected the temporary chairman. The choice of Hill, moreover, was a good one. He had long been a rival of Cleveland in New York politics, and although now allied with sound money men, he had been sympathetic to silver earlier in his career. No doubt he would have gone along with a platform calling for bimetallism through international agreement. But silverites simply could not accept Hill. They had long contended that those who, like McKinley, urged international agreement in place of 16 to 1 were nothing but artful dodgers. Every attempt to establish bimetallism through negotiations with other countries, they pointed out, had come to nought. Furthermore, if Hill were made temporary chairman, the outnumbered Bourbons would be able to influence committee appointments and perhaps control the seating of delegates from contested states. Precedent would have to be overthrown.

After a prolonged debate on the motion to substitute Daniel for Hill, the delegations were polled. The motion passed, 556 to 349, and Chairman Harrity surrendered the gavel to Senator Daniel. Hill and his supporters had to take what comfort they could from the fact that at the moment silver fell short of having a two-thirds majority. The conciliatory note in Daniel's long and platitudinous speech accepting the "high position" to which he had been chosen was inadequate reparation for the indignity Hill had suffered. So was a resolution thanking Harrity for "the able and impartial manner" in which he had presided. But gold men accepted their defeat in silence, and delegates concluded the first day's activity by naming committees.

When the convention reconvened the following morning, the committees were still deliberating behind the scenes. There was nothing to do but mark time. Governor Hogg, Senator Blackburn, Governor

Altgeld, and Massachusetts Congressman George Fred Williams, a recent convert to free coinage, delivered themselves of silver thoughts for the edification and entertainment of the delegates. Finally the Credentials Committee came forward with a partial report. Chairman John H. Atwood, Bryan's friend, announced that after a careful and painstaking comparison of credentials, the Committee had found the roster as prepared by the National Committee correct, except for the delegations from Nebraska and Michigan. The votes of those states, together with an increased number of votes recommended for the District of Columbia and the territories, would give silver its vital two-thirds majority. The report of the Credentials Committee would also accord official recognition as a delegate to William Jennings Bryan. It was adopted enthusiastically, a band started to play, and a triumphant Bryan led his cheering followers to their seats.

The leader of Nebraska silverites did not remain for long on the floor of the Convention. Securing an appointment to the Resolutions Committee, he was soon at work on the phrasing of the platform. With silver forces now in control, delegates expected the Committee on Resolutions to present them with a declaration in favor of free coinage. Word got out, however, that there would be a minority report, and that Bryan would take part in a debate on the money plank. This was one rumor about the Nebraskan that was true (others had hinted that he would be temporary chairman, that he would be permanent chairman, and that he would become Bland's running mate); in fact, Bryan himself had arranged the terms of the debate. Each side would have an hour and twenty minutes. Tillman and Bryan would speak for silver; and Hill, Vilas, and Russell would fight this one last battle for gold.

Tension mounted on the morning of Thursday, July 9, when Senator James K. Jones, Chairman of the Committee on Resolutions, stepped to the rostrum and read the majority report. There were references to Jefferson, justice, and liberty. The paramount importance of the money question was emphasized and the history of the issue sketched. Jones read on: "We demand the free and unlimited coinage of both silver and gold at the present legal ratio of 16 to 1 without waiting for the aid or consent of any other nation." From all over the hall came demands that he read that sentence again. He did so, and then proceeded to the end of the report without interruption. When he finished, the clerk read the minority report calling for maintenance of the gold standard until international agreement on bimetallism could be secured. Senator Jones informed the delegates of the arrangements for the debate and added, "I hope the Convention will listen patiently to what is to be said."

Senator Tillman led off for the silver men with one of his most scorching speeches, and even silver delegates had little patience with the South Carolinian who had wanted to stick his pitchfork into Grover Cleveland's fat ribs. He was sometimes almost incoherent in a tirade that seemed to threaten renewal of sectional hostilities. "We have, instead of a slave oligarchy, a money oligarchy," he shouted. "The one is more insolent than the other was." Repeatedly he was interrupted with hisses and catcalls, and when he finally finished Senator Jones felt constrained to speak in an effort to repair the harm that "Pitchfork Ben" had done. "I simply rose to say," explained Jones, ". . . that I utterly repudiate the charge that this question is sectional."

It was a bad beginning, and the case for silver began to look worse as Senator Hill adroitly presented his arguments. He contended that the Democratic party was the party of sound monetary policy; he pleaded for "the good old principles of Jefferson, of Jackson, of Tilden, of hard money, of safe money." Concluding that if the Democracy kept "in the good old paths of the party" it could win, Hill rested his case. He was followed by Senator Vilas and Governor Russell, who elaborated on the same theme. Russell ended his speech with a prophecy that when the clouds of passion had been rolled away, the protests of the sound money minority would be "hailed as the ark of the covenant of the faith where all Democrats, reunited, may go forth to fight for old principles and carry them to triumphant victory."

It was Bryan's turn. Just before the debate had begun, Clark Howell of the Atlanta *Constitution* had passed him a note. On the back of an envelope he had written: "This is a great opportunity." It was indeed, and no one knew it better than the handsome young orator. "You will not be disappointed," he had scrawled, and had sent the note back. Now the broad jumper from Illinois College bounded to the rostrum. He paused an instant, looking serene and self-possessed, but feeling a slight queasiness in his innards. Crowd noises soon died out as delegates seemed to sense the magnetism of the man who faced them, the suggestion of a smile flickering on his thin lips.

Then he began and the mellow tones of his rich baritone reached to the remotest corners of the giant hall: "I would be presumptuous, indeed, to present myself against the distinguished gentlemen to whom you have listened if this were a mere measuring of abilities; but this is not a contest between persons. The humblest citizen in all the land, when clad in the armor of a righteous cause, is stronger than all the hosts of error." The convention was with him from the very beginning; he was saying what the silver delegates desperately wanted said. The speaker thought of a trained choir as his audience responded instantaneously and in unison to each point he made. "The individual is but an atom; he is born, he acts, he dies; but principles are eternal; and this has been a contest over a principle."

Briefly Bryan traced the growth of the silver movement since that March day in 1895 when the advocates of free coinage had issued an address to the nation declaring the money question paramount. "With a zeal approaching the zeal which inspired the crusaders who followed Peter the Hermit, our silver Democrats went forth from victory unto victory until they are now assembled, not to discuss, not to debate, but to enter up the judgment already rendered by the plain people of this country." William Allen White sat at a telegraph desk in Emporia as the story of the Chicago convention came in on the wire. Ardent Republican that he was, he was moved by fear and rage. But in later years he could write: "It was the first time in my life and in the life of a generation in which any man large enough to lead a national party had boldly and unashamedly made his cause that of the poor and the oppressed."

Turning to the gold delegates, the orator developed his theme in terms they should have been able to understand. "When you come before us and tell us that we are about to disturb your business interests, we reply that you have disturbed our business interests by your course." Now he was getting down to essentials. The wage-earner, "the attorney in a country town," "the merchant at the cross-roads store," "the farmer who goes forth in the morning and toils all day," "the miners who go down a thousand feet into the earth, or climb two thousand feet upon the cliffs"—these too were businessmen, and it was for them that Bryan came to speak.

For whom, did he say? For "the hardy pioneers who have braved all the dangers of the wilderness, who have made the desert to blossom as the rose. . . ." Senator Vilas had called the silver plank a radical scheme and a threat to social order. He had suggested that in the silver movement there might be lurking some unknown Marat, some Danton or Robespierre. Bryan took him to task; he made it clear that if there was a revolutionary force in America, it was the power exercised by organized wealth. Against the encroachments of that power Bryan would stand, as Jackson had stood, in defense of an old and honorable tradition. "We have petitioned, and our petitions have been scorned; we have entreated, and our entreaties have been disregarded; we have begged, and they have mocked when our calamity came. We beg no longer; we entreat no more; we petition no more. We defy them!"

Pacing himself nicely, Bryant turned to a consideration of the platform as a whole. He touched on the income tax and the planks denouncing bank currency and life tenure in office. But it was the money question that really interested him. "If they ask us why it is that we say more on the money question than we say upon the tariff question, I reply that, if protection has slain its thousands, the gold standard has slain its tens of thousands." Middle-of-the-road Populists were arguing that coinage was only one reform among many that should be enacted. Identifying silver with populism, the gold bugs had intimated that the silver platform was dishonest because it did not embody all that its supporters believed. To this Bryan retorted that monetary reform was necessary to all other reforms. Until the "money of the Constitution" had been restored, no other reform could be accomplished.

What were the chances of achieving that essential first reform? Three months ago they had seemed slender indeed. McKinley was the most popular man in the Republican party, and everybody was predicting his election. Now "the man who was once pleased to think that he looked like Napoleon—that man shudders today when he remembers that he was nominated on the anniversary of the battle of Waterloo."

The eloquent young debater did not care on what ground the gold men might choose to fight. Should they argue that gold was good, he would point out to them that they favored bimetallism through international agreement. If gold was so beneficial, why get rid of it? Should they argue that doing favors for the wealthy would benefit everybody, Bryan would answer that the Democratic idea "has been that if you legislate to make the masses prosperous, their prosperity will find its way up through every class which rests upon them." Should they argue that urban sentiment was overwhelmingly for gold, he would reply that "the great cities rest upon our broad and fertile prairies. Burn down your cities and leave our farms, and your cities will spring up again as if by magic; but destroy our farms and the grass will grow in the streets of every city in the country."

Launching into what was to become perhaps the most famous peroration in the history of American political oratory, Bryan thundered:

> Therefore, we care not upon what lines the battle is fought. If they say bimetallism is good, but that we cannot have it until other nations help us, we reply that, instead of having a gold standard because England has, we will restore bimetallism, and then let England have bimetallism because the United States has it. If they dare to come out in the open field and defend the gold standard as a good thing, we will fight them to the uttermost.

> Having behind us the producing masses of this nation and the world, supported by the commercial interests, the laboring interests, and the toilers everywhere, we will answer their demand for a gold standard by saying to them: You shall not press down upon the brow of labor this crown of thorns, you shall not crucify mankind upon a cross of gold.

More than half a century later, when the young men of the Chicago convention had become graybeards and patriarchs, they would recall the speech Bryan made that bright July day in 1896. In all American history there had never been anything like it, they would say. There never would be anything like it. For all its uniqueness, however, the Nebraskan had struck something that Americans liked to think was fundamental and eternal. "The principles upon which Democracy rests are as everlasting as the hills," he had said, "but . . . they must be applied to new conditions as they arise."

Bryan's eloquence crowded every thought out of the minds of the delegates and set reporters to groping for words. It tingled the scalp; it brought tears to the eyes; it took one's breath away. There are demonstrations and demonstrations. Some of the longest on record have been contrived and artificial; the one that followed Bryan's speech lasted only fifteen minutes, but it was the real thing. "From the rear-most wall to the speaker's stand, from end to end of the gigantic hall, came like one great burst of artillery the [response] of the convention," wrote one newsman. Men and women stood on their chairs wildly waving hats, canes, umbrellas, anything that came to hand. "Some, like demented things, divested themselves of their coats and flung them high in the air," reported another observer. "A Texas delegate uprooted the purple standard of his state and bore it frantically to the place where rose the standard of Nebraska. In a twinkling others followed his example." Bryan himself was surrounded by ardent well-wishers. A reporter from the Chicago *Daily News* thought he looked "bewildered, half-frightened, panting, yet proud and satisfied" as he fought to keep from being crushed.

It was, for many, the high point of the convention and the campaign. But the convention had much unfinished business to attend to. By a vote of 628 to 301 it adopted the majority report and proceeded at once to the naming of candidates. When the roll of the states was called, Senator Jones of Arkansas yielded to Senator Vest of Missouri who, in nominating Bland, read a silly jingle that was a measure of the anticlimax following the "Cross of Gold" speech:

> Give us Silver Dick, and Silver quick,
> And we will make McKinley sick
> In the ides of next November.

In presenting Bryan, Henry T. Lewis of Georgia told the delegates that to honor the Nebraskan would be to honor themselves: "nominate him and you will reflect credit upon the party you represent. . . ." Other candidates placed in nomination were Governor Matthews, Governor Boies, Senator Blackburn, John R. McLean, Governor Pattison of Pennsylvania, and Governor Pennoyer of Oregon.

Although Bryan's speech had captivated silver delegates, the convention was still apparently wide open when balloting began the next day, July 10. On the first ballot Bland had 235 votes to 137 for Bryan. They were followed by Pattison (the gold men who felt like voting at all voted for him), Blackburn, Boies, McLean, and Matthews. On the next two ballots, both Bland and Bryan increased their vote; going into the fourth, Bland led 291 to 219. Then came the break that many delegates had expected and Bryan men had hoped for. On the fourth ballot the Nebraskan led Bland 280 to 241. After the secretary had announced the totals, Governor Stone read a letter he had received from Bland two or three days before: "I wish it to be understood that I do not desire the nomination unless it is the judgment of the free silver delegates that I would be the strongest candidate." The Democracy nominated William Jennings Bryan on the fifth ballot.

Vice Presidential candidates are usually either faceless and innocuous or they are potential troublemakers someone wants to put in cold storage. Arthur Sewall, chosen by Democrats on the fifth and final day of their convention, was not a troublemaker, nor was he a man who required office of any kind to make his reputation. He belonged to a long-established New England family that had developed Bath, Maine, into one of the principal shipbuilding ports of the nineteenth century. As the head of his own firm Sewall built, owned, and operated more sailing vessels than any other man in America after the Civil War. His executive ability led him into banking and railroading as well as shipbuilding; he was associated with the Eastern Railroad, the Central Railroad, and the Boston and Maine. As a Democrat he was by Maine standards—and those of his own family—a maverick in politics.

Sewall had served on the National Committee, but when he voted against Hill for temporary chairman the Maine delegation removed him from that position. He telegraphed his wife that he had now left politics for good. Thirty-six hours later he was named as candidate for the Vice Presidency over such contenders as Richard P. Bland, Joseph Sibley, George Fred Williams, and John R. McLean. Did the Democrats make a mistake? Some people thought so. But that is a part of the 1896 story which must be discussed in its proper context.

In the meantime William Jennings Bryan made his triumphal return to Lincoln by way of Salem, St. Louis, and Kansas City. The capital city of Nebraska was appropriately made up for the homecoming. Party lines disappeared momentarily as people decorated their houses and public buildings with bunting, floral displays, and here and there incandescent lights. Nebraskans were proud of what the eloquent young man had accomplished. At least some of them were. The hostile Omaha *Bee* interjected a discordant note when it printed a comment from the Louisville *Courier-Journal:* "The league of free silver men who set to work several months ago to capture the organization of the democratic party has accomplished its purpose. It has put forth, in the democratic name, a platform which violates almost every cardinal democratic tenet, and has nominated as the democratic leader a young hot-head, who but recently abandoned the democratic for the populistic party." Before the campaign was over the discordant note would swell into a shrill crescendo.

VII

THE DISAPPOINTED

ON JULY 4, 1896, AS DEMOCRATS IN CHICAGO WERE PREparing for the climactic showdown between gold and silver factions, the Socialist Labor party opened its ninth annual convention at the Grand Central Palace in New York City. Unlike the GOP and the Democracy it did not defer to traditional American myths and values. Unlike the two major parties it did not have much of a following. The large hall was almost empty when National Secretary Henry Kuhn called the first session to order. Less than a hundred delegates and only a few newspapermen and spectators were on hand later when Comrade Kuhn read the report of the National Executive Committee.

As if to compensate for the party's national insignificance, the report began with a survey of world-wide successes of the working class movement. "Wherever we look, we see the Socialist movement forging ahead, in England as in France, in Belgium, Germany, Austria, Italy and the Scandinavian countries," read the Secretary. "Even in far-off Australia, even in Argentina, our comrades are sowing the seed, and who knows but that the latest participant in the capitalist St. Vitus' dance—Japan—may not soon witness the first manifestation of the spirit of Socialism." So much for conditions abroad. The bulk of the report surveyed conditions at home.

Looking back over the last three years, the executive committee could "attest steady and healthy progress" in the United States too. Happily, "that particular back-number form of a labor organization, the pure and simple trade union" was on the decline. During the unrest of recent years the capitalist class had been safely sheltered. The courts, the army, and prisons had all been employed for its protection. The result had been disillusionment with "fakir-ridden" labor organizations such as the Knights of Labor. Workers were beginning to see that their interests could best be advanced by the Socialist Trade and Labor Alliance.

In the area of politics it was evident that the tariff issue had become a dead letter, "much to the sorrow of capitalist politicians, who never had a better means of befuddling the minds of workingmen." The party of Jefferson seemed ready to burst from the pressures exerted upon it, while the GOP had become the party of "capitalism par excellence." With obvious satisfaction the executive committee ventured a political prediction: "The People's Party will have the wind taken out of its sails by the silver development in the Democratic camp; it will be stripped of its Socialistic pretensions as soon as there is a chance to attain increased strength along the lines of its true character as a middle class movement; it will cease to stand in our way and hinder the growth of our party in Western States, where the allurements held out by Populist politicians served to give them quite a large following from among the working class." And what would be the result of this demise of the People's party? "The lines will be drawn much clearer and more distinct, and it will be easier for men to know on what side of the fence they really belong."

The attack on Populism was nothing new; from its very beginning Marxian radicals had been sniping away at the party. They had always condemned it as agrarian and middle class. Yet their polemics seemed unfair and inconsistent, for the program of the People's party and the program of the Socialist Labor party were in some significant respects similar. Populists had long ago incorporated into their Omaha platform radical measures (such as the demand for public ownership of railroads and utilities) which indicated their willingness to alter the basic structure of the American economy.

There was good reason for the envy which inspired the Socialist attacks. Growing out of the Farmers' Alliance, the People's party was primarily an agrarian movement and it would remain an agrarian movement to the end of its days. Something about it, however, attracted men who felt that American society had fallen short of its promise. Single taxers for a time entertained some notion of using the party to achieve their ends. Prohibitionists, demanding government control over alcoholic beverages, viewed with favor a movement which made no secret of its desire to expand government controls. Jacob Coxey saw no reason why Populists should not support his public works schemes. Labor leaders had been conspicuous in Populist conferences and conventions, as had Bellamy nationalists. Silver men sought to maintain contacts with the movement. The party did, indeed, hold out allurements which were attractive to the working class and to reformers. And it produced a radicalism that sought to avoid both traditional myths and Marxism, a radicalism that sought its justification in economic realities.

One of the most important of the reformers who joined the People's party was Henry Demarest Lloyd, a Chicago journalist who had long been concerned with what he regarded as the failure of the American economy to achieve industrial justice. In 1894 he published *Wealth Against Commonwealth,* a devastating indictment of trusts in general and Standard Oil in particular. One of the earliest and best examples of what later came to be called muckraking literature, the book appeared at a time when Lloyd was beginning to view the People's party as a most promising agency for correcting the evils of industrial capitalism.

During the campaign of 1894 Lloyd worked hard to effect a coalition of workers and Populists in Illinois. "The People's party is a middle class party," he admitted in *Arbeiter Zeitung;* "a permanent union of the working men with it might prove . . . unprofitable, as it contains too many doubtful and unprogressive elements." Yet he persuaded himself that "a closer union of the industrial workers with the more advanced farmers" was essential. At a conference held in Springfield in July, 1894, Lloyd managed to secure agreement among labor union leaders, single taxers, socialists, farmers, and assorted radicals to support the Populist state ticket in the coming election.

One of the highlights of the campaign was an address which Lloyd, himself a candidate for Congress, delivered at a rally in Chicago's Central Music Hall on October 6. It was a memorable event, and it was widely reported in the press. Clarence Darrow, a young lawyer from Kinsman, Ohio, presided over the meeting, and the venerable Lyman Trumbull, with whom Bryan had studied law, was one of the principal speakers. Darrow had resigned as chief counsel of the Chicago and Northwestern Railroad in order to defend Eugene V. Debs, and he enjoyed immense popularity with workers. Trumbull, the champion of equal rights, had broken his political association with the Democratic party as he had earlier broken with the Republicans. Three thousand strong, workers, Populists, and reformers packed the hall.

In his address—one of the most significant in the history of the Populist movement—Lloyd summarized his hopes and convictions and established himself as one of the principal philosophers of Populist radicalism. "The appearance at the polls of a new party, which was not known in 1888, and in 1892, in its first presidential campaign, cast over 1,000,000 votes, is a hint that a new conception of reform is shaping itself in the minds of our fellow citizens," he told his cheering audience. "They want reform that will reform, and they want it now." Conservatives might caution delay, as they had in France on the eve of the Revolution and as they always did when any great social movement threatened the status quo. But "no great idea is ever lost." Democracy, "the greatest of human ideas," was moving from victory to victory throughout the world. The great political fact of the time was the formation of parties "to democratize the millionaire, and, as Jefferson did when he democratized the provincial patricians of Virginia, to do it as nearly as possible at one sitting."

Taking a broad view of the reforms advocated by new parties in Europe, Australia, and America, Lloyd found them fundamentally the same. They all opposed an inequitable distribution of the profits of industry. "The millions produce wealth; only the tens have it," he observed. "There is the root of the whole matter. The first and last political issue of our time is with its concentrated wealth. Not with wealth, but with its concentration." Of course those who pointed out the evils which resulted from such concentration—contraction of the currency, monopoly, pauperism, the tyranny of corporations, the corruption of governments, the congestion of cities—were denounced as calamity howlers. Yet "when strong, shrewd, grasping, coveteous men devote themselves to creating calamities, fortunate are the people who are awakened by faithful calamity howlers."

Men talked about the coming revolution, but a revolution had already come. The way in which government had been used to enrich a few was a revolution. The creation of railroad millionaires was a revolution. Granting special privileges and property to street-railway syndicates, gas companies, and power companies was a revolution. Allowing corporation presidents and managers to "go free of all punishment for the crimes they are committing" was a revolution. Permitting great corporations to monopolize entire markets was a revolution. This was not the end. "The last and deepest and greatest revolution of all is that by which the mines, machinery, factories, currency, land, entrusted to private hands as private property, only as a stewardship, to warm, feed, clothe, serve mankind, are used to make men cold, hungry, naked, and destitute."

No wonder a counterrevolution was being organized through people's parties all over the world. "Chicago today leads the van in this great forward movement," said Lloyd with some pride. "Here the workingmen, capitalists, single-taxers, and socialists have come together to join forces with each other and with the farmers, as has been done in no other city." The people were beginning to insist upon the principle for which workingmen of Illinois had stood firm as a rock: "the principle that they have the right at their option to own and operate collectively any or all of the means of production, distribution, and exchange." The democratization of government and of collective industry was part of "one great upward emancipation." The legitimate offspring and successor of the republic was the cooperative commonwealth.

The people could not look to the two established parties for relief. Perhaps Republican and Democratic organizations had served a purpose, but now their work was done. They were responsible for the "pandemonium of intermittent panic" which plagued the country, and to vote for them was to vote for "more panics, more pandemoniums." There was hope, however. "There is a party that the people can trust because in the face of overwhelming odds, without distinguished leaders, money, office, or prestige, it has raised the standard of a principle to save the people." No halfway measures would do. "The continual refrain of Mommsen, the great historian of Rome, is that liberties and prosperity were lost because its reformers were only half reformers, and none of its statesmen would strike at the root of its evils."

This could never be said of the People's party, for its program did go to the root of industrial evils in America. The people would eliminate monopoly. They would control judges, president, and representatives. "The same constitution that could take the property of unwilling citizens for the railroads for rights-of-way can take the railroads, willing or unwilling, to be the nation's property when the people come in." So it was with money too. "The same constitution that could demonetize silver can remonetize it, or demonetize gold for a better money than either." There would be postal savings banks for the people and low street-car fares on lines owned by the people. Municipal power plants would provide electricity to brighten all the dark places of American cities. Public housing projects and cooperative colonies would spring into existence. "Every man who works will get a living and every man who gets a living shall work, when the people come in."

Clearly Lloyd hoped to achieve much more than countervailing power for workers and farmers within the capitalistic structure. What he wanted was a root and branch reform of the American economy. Those captivated by his vision were ready to join in a really radical movement which would attempt to solve problems of the industrial age by introducing fundamental changes in the economic structure. Back in 1891 the Lincoln, Nebraska, *Farmers' Alliance* had defined the Populist position: "The people's party has sprung into existence not to make the black man free, but to emancipate all men; not to secure political freedom to a class, but to gain for all *industrial* freedom, without which there can be no political freedom; no lasting people's government." To this point of view Henry Demarest Lloyd gave cogent expression, developing his arguments with subtlety and skill.

Whether or not Lloyd's ideas represented a consensus within Populism may be open to question. There is no doubt, however, that Populists looked with favor upon the concerted action of farmers and workers. One of Ignatius Donnelly's correspondents thought that "the real producers of the country are simply the helpless slaves of the money power, which is forcing them into a worse condition of servitude each year." He believed that "if they could only be firmly united together, monopoly would have to succumb, or else seek some more fruitful field—but can such a thing be accomplished?" That was the vital question.

As a matter of fact significant steps toward a Populist-labor coalition had already been taken in several states at the time Lloyd delivered his Music Hall address in 1894. As early as September, 1893, the Wisconsin Labor Congress had endorsed the platform of the People's party. The next year the Wisconsin State Federation of Labor had placed itself on record as supporting the Populists. And on the Fourth of July the state convention of the People's party had returned the favor by adopting the entire political program of the

American Federation of Labor along with the Omaha platform. Even the Milwaukee Socialists had been drawn into the Wisconsin People's party. Similar coalitions had been formed in New York and Minnesota. In Minneapolis and St. Paul, trade unionists and Socialists had joined the Populist party in such numbers that the Socialist Labor party had been decimated.

Certainly those who saw some hope of an effective farmer-labor movement were not indulging in vague pipe dreams. Yet difficulties had to be surmounted before a coalition could be formed on a national scale. One of the principal obstacles to unity in Illinois had been "Plank 10" of a platform which had been proposed by T. J. Morgan, a Chicago machinist of socialist proclivities, and which was then being discussed by the American Federation of Labor. The controversial measure demanded "the collective ownership by the people of all means of production and distribution"; its adoption by the Populists would have committed them to socialism. It was further than most agrarians in the party were ready to go, and they had rejected it. "If this is what you came to the people's party for, we don't want you," National Chairman Herman E. Taubeneck had told labor leaders in 1894. "Go back from where you came with your socialism."

Working desperately—realistically—for unity among reform factions and radical groups, Lloyd had produced a compromise formula tying collective ownership to the initiative and referendum. Populists had been willing to pledge themselves "to the principles of the collective ownership by the people of all such means of production and distribution *as the people elect* to operate for the commonwealth." The modification had made possible at least temporary labor-farmer cooperation.

Ultimately, however, the Illinois coalition failed, and a national organization of farmers and workers never materialized. Samuel Gompers had been a consistent opponent of Plank 10, and he proposed to fight its adoption by the American Federation of Labor when the union held its convention in Denver in December, 1894. Lloyd pleaded with him not to do so; it would mean shattering the foundation on which the Illinois coalition had been constructed and therefore the foundation on which a national coalition might be built. "What is needed in my view," wrote Lloyd in August, "is a delegate assembly of all the reform elements to give immediate direction and concentration to the acts of the coming election." Only with the help of the American Federation of Labor could the right kind of farmer-labor movement be established on a national scale. "Such a convention should make terms for the working men with the People's party and the Socialist Labour party and the Single-Taxers that would be equal to the fruits of ten years of agitation." The time had come, he argued, for leaders to assert themselves for the good of all men. "The people are scattered, distracted, leaderless, waiting for just such guidance. And the opportunity will not recur."

Nevertheless Gompers spurned the appeal. What Lloyd had in mind was at odds with his whole philosophy of labor. He would be partisan to principles, but he wished to avoid party entanglements. His union might function more effectively as a pressure group, he thought, than as part of a farmer-labor coalition. Beyond this, Gompers had no interest in espousing socialist ideas whether tied to the initiative and referendum or not. Some time later he would tell his socialist colleagues: "Economically, you are unsound; socially, you are wrong; industrially, you are an impossibility." He did not feel quite as strongly as that in 1894, but he still wanted nothing to do with Plank 10. He resorted to every parliamentary maneuver he could think of, and he brought to bear every pressure at his command. He succeeded in getting the offensive plank defeated. Even though he himself was ousted as president of the Union, he did secure his major objective.

The action taken by the American Federation of Labor was a serious setback to the cause of farmer-labor unity. Lloyd did not give up hope, but it was evident that he and others who favored basic changes in the American economy now faced mounting opposition. It was true that James K. Sovereign, head of the Knights of Labor, became a member of the Executive Committee of the People's party. Eugene V. Debs also became identified with Populism.

But Sovereign's organization was deteriorating, and Debs was so involved in litigation resulting from the Pullman strike that, as he wrote James B. Weaver in 1894, "the pressure of duties on me at this time prevent my lending you a helping hand." How much the support of the American Federation of Labor might have meant was by no means clear; that group was still in the formative stage of its development. Furthermore, the Populists were not all of one mind. Agrarian leaders were themselves too divided in their counsels to achieve effective union with urban workers. Yet who could tell what might have happened had radicals and reformers chosen to move in the direction suggested by Lloyd?

If a farmer-labor coalition seemed difficult if not impossible to achieve, no one in the People's party questioned the desirability of unity. Populists only questioned on what grounds unity of working men, farmers, and reformers might be secured. The organizational success of the silver movement stood out in marked contrast to the abortive effort to bring farmers and workers into a grand reform alliance. It was both an object lesson and a temptation to Populist radicals. Shortly after the election of 1894 H. E. Taubeneck promised to organize immediately for the campaign of 1896, and he added significantly, "We shall, more than likely, confine ourselves to the money question in the future, and make that the test of party fealty." The broad program of reform was not to be repudiated, but silver was to be emphasized for the sake of unity. In December, 1894, a Populist conference in St. Louis reaffirmed the Omaha platform; it did not, however, reverse the trend toward silver.

Early in 1895 the New York *World* polled Populist and silver leaders, asking whether or not a new party would be established on the basis of financial reform. Senator Tillman thought the organization of a new party inevitable. Adoniram J. Warner, expressing the view of the Bimetallic League, said that "there is now in this country but one issue, and on that but two parties, the Gold Party and the Bimetallic Party." Taubeneck, who had already committed himself, agreed. "The People's Party at its next National Convention will declare in favor of making the money question the 'great central idea,' with no other planks except those which add strength to this one," he said. "Those who desire to retard monetary reform by loading us down with other issues will, with the Socialists and Communists, go to the rear."

Some Populists differed emphatically with their national chairman. "A party with only one plank, and that confined to silver," said M. W. Howard, Populist Congressman from Alabama, "would be so weak that it would not control a single electoral vote." William A. Peffer thought that a new party would be formed, "but it will be built on a foundation deeper and broader than 'free silver' or 'bimetallism,' for these terms express nothing that reaches the core of the troubles which confront us." Thomas E. Watson did not think a new party would be formed, but he did believe that "an understanding will be reached between the Populists, the American Bimetallic Party, and the free-silver elements of the Democratic and Republican parties." He believed "a union of all the anti-class elements is absolutely necessary."

Such men as Howard, Peffer, and Watson were middle-of-the-road Populists. So firmly did they believe in the broad reform program outlined in the Omaha platform that they were extremely reluctant to compromise. James B. Weaver believed in the Omaha platform too; he had, after all, campaigned on it. But long before most of his fellow Populists he saw that silver provided the basis of united action. "In my judgment," he said in response to the *World's* question, "there will be an alliance—not fusion—formed between now and the coming of the campaign in 1896, made up of Populists, Democrats, and Republicans." The suggestion that all those who favored reform should agree on silver was in Weaver's view a crucial one. "If the kindred but now divided factions shall have the good judgment to accept and act upon the timely suggestion—stripping themselves for the time being of everything else, no matter how important—they will close the century with the greatest battle ever fought and crown it with the greatest victory ever won for commercial supremacy and industrial freedom."

If there was disagreement within the People's party, it was a disagreement not on fundamentals but on political strategy. The middle-of-the-roaders of course wished to stand by the platform; they could not regard silver as anything more than a minor matter. The Taubeneck-Weaver view was that the People's party could first establish its control over all those groups favoring free silver and then, having secured that reform, move on to others. Weaver and Taubeneck obviously predicated their strategy on the assumption that the Populist party would be able to establish its ascendency over all silver and reform organizations.

That assumption did not appear to be altogether without foundation early in 1896. On New Year's Day William Jennings Bryan wrote letters to Weaver, Donnelly, Clarence Darrow, Marion Butler, and other Populist leaders. He argued that "success in the next campaign can only be secured by the consolidation of the silver sentiment upon the same presidential ticket." How such consolidation could be brought about was not at the moment entirely certain, but he pointed out an interesting possibility. "I think it is of vital importance that the populist convention shall not be held until after the democratic and republican conventions," he wrote. "It can then take advantage of the errors of the old parties. Wise action will be much more probable if the convention meets at such a time as to be able to take a survey of the whole field and understand all the conditions."

Butler, for one, agreed with Bryan that silver men should unite. "There is no hope for silver or for the people in any other course in the near future," he commented in his reply. He even asked Bryan for an estimate of how many silver states would bolt the Democratic national convention when it nominated a gold man for President. Other members of the National Committee were persuaded that the party stood to gain from silverite defections from the two major parties. They appointed a coordinating committee to meet with leaders of the Bimetallic League in Washington on January 22 and they gave it power to set the time and place for the party's national convention. As noted in the last chapter, Populists and silverites agreed to hold simultaneous conventions in St. Louis beginning July 22—after Republicans and Democrats had chosen candidates and declared themselves on the money question.

When spring came and proponents of silver won victory after victory in Democratic state conventions, the hope that silver men would come trooping into the People's party began to fade. Yet even as late as the middle of May, Taubeneck was predicting that gold bugs would control both Republican and Democratic conventions. "It seems to me," he wrote Donnelly on the 15th, "that at no time since our party was organized have the prospects for a great victory been so flattering as today." Taubeneck was deluding himself. Weaver was more realistic when he wrote Bryan on May 29: "Should the silver men be able to control the Chicago convention both as to platform and nominations be careful to have the platform cover the entire money question: second let your nominations be advisory simply and not final." This, he thought, would provide an opportunity to confer with Populists and silverites in St. Louis and keep open the possibility of union.

Dyed-in-the-wool Populists could not but have some doubts about the course of events. "The only fear I now have . . ." wrote one of them to Ignatius Donnelly, "is that both the old parties are going to stampede, frightened by the red flag of the free-silverites, and land their putrescent old carcasses in the 'middle of the road' where we have traveled since 1892." Shortly before Democrats convened in Chicago, William A. Peffer commented upon recent developments and what they might mean. He was sure that Democrats would incorporate a silver plank in their platform and nominate a silver candidate. Nevertheless he did not think "existing conditions warrant populist endorsement of the democratic presidential ticket." He said he had hoped "that there might be some amalgamation of democrats, populists, silver men and all others in a new declaration of principles, and, if need be, a new name. But the time for that has gone by and all that remains is for the populist party to maintain its integrity by nominating its own candidates on its own platform."

When the Democratic convention was over and Bryan had been

nominated, Populists found themselves facing distasteful alternatives. It was obvious that many who were in sympathy with Populist principles would now support the Democratic candidate. But could the People's party itself support him? Could a fusion with Democrats be effected? If so, what would fusion mean? Populists were as divided as most of them were disgruntled. "The Democratic party never has dealt honestly with the people in the past, and cannot be expected to change its record now," asserted the *Southern Mercury.* The paper conceded that "Mr. Bryan is a very gifted man, but he is in very bad company." The platform, which contained several Populist planks and yet did not incorporate the whole Populist program, was a product of Democratic perfidy. It was entirely inconsistent with the party's record; the stolen planks had been put in only to catch votes. What should good Populists do now? The *Southern Mercury* cast its advice in doggerel:

> Fusion may do for the spoil hunting lot,
> And comfort the democratic crew;
> But if we're true coin, no fusion we'll join,
> But paddle [our] own canoe.

Others could certainly sympathize, but much as they would have liked to paddle their own canoe, they could not do so. Henry Demarest Lloyd stated their dilemma succinctly: "If we fuse, we are sunk; if we don't fuse, all the silver men we have will leave us for the more powerful Democrats." Populists were understandably disappointed in the choices they would have to make in St. Louis. "Exciting times there," Ignatius Donnelly noted in his diary as he speculated on possible alternatives. "I like Bryan, but I do not feel that we can safely adopt the Dem. candidates. I fear it will be the end of our party."

Although the Populist convention was not scheduled to begin until Wednesday, July 22, delegates began to arrive in large numbers on the previous weekend. Some of them walked to save train fare. Some could afford rooms in only the shoddiest hotels. Some bought nickel meals at cheap lunch counters. Most of them were, like Donnelly, in a grim and somber mood. The usual assortment of reformers, political opportunists, and cranks, along with silver Republicans and silver Democrats, was on the scene to plead for special causes. It was as contentious a group as had yet assembled in 1896, and the Omaha *Bee* predicted that it would be "the stormiest political gathering of the year." The prediction was amply justified.

Two days before the opening session of the convention, party leaders anxiously discussed various possibilities. However disagreeable endorsement of the Democratic ticket and platform may have been, some believed that Populists had no other choice. Others continued to demand that the party draw up its own platform and name its own candidates. Between those two extremes there were several shades of opinion.

In general the southerners were more reluctant to compromise and fuse than were northerners. To leave the party of white supremacy in the South was to become a pariah. Southern Populist leaders not only had left the party, but also were working to form combinations and alliances that violated every prejudice of those who dominated southern opinion. Instead of mouthing platitudinous phrases about the glories of a reconstituted union—phrases which obscured the facts of economic subservience to the Northeast and of racial inequality—Populists spoke of uniting the South and the West against the East. Instead of discussing the achievements of industrial development, they talked about a coalition of farmers and urban laborers. Instead of accepting assumptions of white supremacy, they sought an understanding with Negroes. Southern Populists, in other words, had violated southern taboos, and they were made to pay the price in social ostracism and economic discrimination. Having sacrificed much for the sake of their party, they desperately hoped that it would maintain its integrity.

For westerners, on the other hand, changing party affiliations was seldom the traumatic experience it was for southerners. "I care not for party names," said Jerry Simpson, "it is the substance we are after, and we have it with William J. Bryan." Most of the western

Populists agreed. Such men labored to produce a compromise between fusionists and middle-roaders, and they entertained many suggestions. Perhaps the most common was that Populists name their own candidates but combine with Democrats on fusion electoral tickets. Then after the election all silver electors would be in a position to support the stronger man for President and the weaker for Vice President.

Party leaders could come to no agreement before the convention met, however, and by Wednesday excitement was running high. The only major action of the first day was the selection of a temporary chairman, and Senator Marion Butler was chosen by acclamation. His name had been submitted by the National Committee as one who could best unite different factions of the party. A southerner, Butler shared the conviction that Populists should retain their identity, but he also favored Bryan's nomination. "It has been a part of my experience that, whenever you see some good men going to one extreme and other good men going to the other extreme," he said in his keynote address, "the path of truth lies between them."

Nothing had been decided, but middle-of-the-roaders hoped to gain control of the convention that evening. They had planned an impressive demonstration, thinking that it might turn back the movement toward fusion. But the demonstration never came off. When delegates assembled at eight o'clock, there were no lights. Although they tried to make do with candles, no one could work up much enthusiasm in the darkened hall. Recalling that deliberately turning out the lights was nothing new in political conventions, the middle-roaders claimed there had been foul play. However that may have been, it was the last chance they had to dominate the proceedings.

The next morning fusionists were in control. That became evident in the struggle over permanent organization, when two reports were submitted. A majority of the committee favored Senator William V. Allen of Nebraska, a strong fusion man and friend of Bryan, for permanent chairman. The minority report named James E. Campion, who was a middle-roader but not very well known. The vote for adopting the majority report was 758 to 564, a good measure of fusionist as opposed to middle-road strength. Fusionists also won significant victories with the seating of Byran delegates from contested states and with the appointment of James B. Weaver to the chairmanship of the resolutions committee.

In thanking the convention for "this distinguished mark of confidence and esteem," Allen said that his selection as permanent chairman had come as a surprise and that he had not prepared a speech. But the Senator had once filibustered for almost fifteen hours against repeal of the Sherman Silver Purchase Act, and he was not one to hold his tongue for lack of preparation. At the conclusion of his rambling remarks, he told the delegates that he was not there to advocate Bryan's nomination. "It is for you to choose and not for me," he said. "If by putting a third ticket in the field you would defeat free coinage; defeat a withdrawal of the issue power of national banks; defeat Government ownership of railroads, telephones and telegraphs; defeat an income tax and foist gold monometallism and high taxation upon the people for a generation to come, which would you do?"

The logic was tortured, but the point was clear enough. Allen was for Bryan. When he went back to Nebraska, he wanted to be able to say that "all the great doctrines we have advocated for years, have been made possible by your action." He did not want the voters to say that "when the first ray of light appeared and the people were looking with expectancy and with anxiety for relief, the party was not equal to the occasion; that it was stupid; it was blind; it kept 'in the middle of the road,' and missed the golden opportunity."

With Allen duly installed as permanent chairman, fusionists stood poised to take full advantage of the golden opportunity. But there were some surprises to come; Populists had been shocked by the course of events, and no one could predict how the convention would act. Conceding for the moment that Byran would probably be nominated, the middle-road faction concentrated its efforts against Sewall. The shipbuilder, banker, railroad director was no fit candidate for the People's party, they argued. And since the vice-presidential nomination was so important, they asked, why not reverse the usual order and name a vice-presidential candidate first? It was a bright idea, and the convention began to buzz with excitement. The procedure was embodied in a minority report of the rules committee; and after a muddled roll call during which there was much shifting of votes, it became apparent that the unorthodox order would be followed.

Now there was disorder among the fusionists. Not even the adoption of a platform which emphasized silver could restore their confidence. Middle-roaders once more took heart. Perhaps the Democrats could be persuaded to withdraw Sewall. Perhaps Bryan would refuse to be considered for the nomination and Populists could name a man of their own choice. In any event there would be a good strong Populist running for Vice President on the People's party ticket.

Senator James K. Jones, Bryan's campaign manager, was in St. Louis looking after Democratic interests and exerting every possible effort to win delegates over to fusion. When he learned of the decision to nominate a vice-presidential candidate first, he sent Bryan a hurried telegram suggesting that he withdraw if the Populists rejected Sewall. The Nebraskan agreed. "Withdraw my name if Sewall is not nominated," he wired back. For good measure he sent the same message to Allen. At this point there was a breakdown in communications between Jones and Allen. Jones gave out an announcement describing Bryan's position and quoting his telegram. Allen, on the other hand, ignored the message. He not only refused to read it to the convention, but he also denied that he had even received it.

If the Jones announcement sounded like an ultimatum, Populists refused to be intimidated. On Friday evening they went ahead with nominating speeches for vice-presidential candidates. Sewall was named with support from ultrafusionists. Middle-roaders did not concentrate on a single candidate; Harry Skinner of North Carolina, Frank Burkett of Mississippi, A. L. Mimms of Tennessee, and Mann Page of Virginia were all placed in nomination. The candidate who had the strongest support, however, was Thomas E. Watson. The backers of the middle-road Georgian were exceptionally shrewd. They apparently led him to believe that should he be nominated the Democrats would withdraw Sewall, and with that understanding Watson agreed to be a candidate with Bryan. The Watson candidacy thus had a certain appeal to the compromise-minded, and in the early morning hours of Saturday, July 25, he was nominated for Vice President. A majority of the Populists, as Donnelly put it in his speech seconding Watson's nomination, were "willing to swallow Democracy gilded with the genius of a Bryan" but were unwilling to "stomach plutocracy in the body of Sewall."

After a few hours' rest, delegates reconvened for the last day's sessions. They were tired and somewhat bewildered; after seemingly endless debate and struggle their nerves were frayed. Now in the closing hours of the convention, when the party would name a presidential candidate, the position of the extreme middle-roaders was weak. They had no one to name. Not a single member of the middle-road faction could command a respectable following. Colonel S. F. Norton was finally chosen as the only candidate to oppose Bryan's nomination. Norton enjoyed some prestige as the author of *Ten Men of Money Island,* but his candidacy was impromptu and poorly organized.

Bryan, on the other hand, received support from some of the big names of the party. He was nominated by Weaver and seconded by Taubeneck, Simpson, Donnelly, and Mrs. Lease. Of course there was some question about whether or not he would accept the nomination if it were tendered. While the votes were being tallied, a rumor ran through the hall that Allen had received a telegram from Bryan requesting that his name be withdrawn. When questioned about the telegram, Allen denied receiving it. Governor Stone, Missouri's Democratic chief executive, was there at the time, and he asked permission to read a message which he had received from Bryan. Allen refused, explaining that a Democratic communication could have no bearing on Populist decisions. Thus so far as Populists were concerned Bryan was still a candidate, and he was nominated on the first ballot. The final vote stood 1,042 for Bryan to 321 for Norton.

Recognizing that Bryan might well refuse the nomination, the convention gave the national committee plenary power to act as it saw fit should such a contingency arise.

The outcome of the People's party convention stimulated endless discussion. Everybody had an opinion. Henry Demarest Lloyd, writing in *The Review of Reviews,* thought a serious mistake had been made, but he was charitable. "The solicitude to do nothing which should hinder the Rising of the People, if that had really begun," he wrote, "was the motive that led to the indorsement of Bryan." If radical leaders had quietly accepted the platform which said much less than they would have liked, and if they went along with the nomination of Bryan, it was because they believed that only through fusion could radical hopes be kept alive.

Lloyd was highly critical of Taubeneck and others who had led the fight for fusion (even though he himself recognized that the party had little choice). His views were echoed by the *Southern Mercury,* which made the Chairman a scapegoat: "When the national committee placed the national convention after the dates set for holding the old party conventions the first move on the chessboard was made that rendered it impracticable for the reformers to win the game. Placing the young and vigorous peoples party at the tail end of the procession robbed it of every advantage of position, and made it the Lazarus begging at the gates of the old party Dives." Some middle-roaders wanted to repudiate the action taken at St. Louis. "By all that is high and holy use your best efforts to get a new ticket in the field," wrote a Californian to Donnelly, "a straight ticket with, if possible, yourself as the head and Debs as your mate will carry the country by storm and save our honor."

On the other hand, some middle-roaders were ready to cooperate with Democrats in the fullest degree. "Mr. Bryan stands for the people—as Lincoln did," commented the Topeka *Advocate* after the Populist convention. "Voters without respect to party are gathering about him, determined to lend themselves in this supreme crisis to the one great object of defeating the movement to fasten upon the country a gold basis for our circulating medium." The *Advocate* went so far as to say that there was no good reason why Bryan should be expected to either accept or decline the People's party nomination. He needed all the votes he could get, and he should not be embarrassed by "any sort of demands beyond good faith." Populists should freely and willingly give him their support, for "the defeat of McKinley will be the victory of Populists."

If middle-roaders were for the most part dissatisfied with the results of the Populist convention, the fusionists were not exactly elated. Their most common criticism was directed at Watson's nomination. S. P. Van Patten, an alternate delegate from Arkansas, wrote to George H. Schilling, a friend of Altgeld and of labor, describing the confusion and uncertainty that had prevailed that night when Populists were nominating a vice-presidential candidate. "All this muddle was caused by the fool nomination of Tom Watson," he asserted. "I am satisfied that Mark Hanna engineered it and that the *middle xxx etc.* [*sic*] leaders were fixed before the convention met." Speaking for silverites *The National Bimetallist* contended that the naming of Watson was a mistake. The autonomy of the People's party did not require it, for the party still had its own state organizations. The *Bimetallist* was confident that Bryan would be elected, "but any complications growing out of the Vice-Presidential 'mix-up' will have the effect of encouraging the enemy and stimulating him to renewed effort."

The Watson nomination did place Bryan in an awkward dilemma which was to cause him anxiety during the campaign. Yet most delegates, including some who favored fusion, were less concerned with Bryan's problems than with the fate of their party. Their interest in Populist reforms influenced their dealings with the silver convention meeting in St. Louis at the same time. Although a conference committee was formed, Populists refused privileges of the floor to members of the Silver party. According to Lloyd, they "listened with unconcealed impatience to every reference to the silver body." Nevertheless the silver men went about their business. They nominated Bryan and Sewall and adopted the Democratic platform. The Silver party did not merge with the Democracy, for it felt that it could perform a useful function as an independent organization. It might attract the votes of those who were reluctant to cast their ballots for the Democratic party.

To the end a majority of Populists could not view silver as anything but a minor issue. Yet the tide of events ran against them and created one of the supreme ironies of the campaign of 1896. "A party which hates Democracy accepted the Democratic nominee," wrote Lloyd, "and a party which has no faith in silver as a panacea accepted silver practically as the sole issue of the campaign." No doubt Populists were justified in their disappointment. They were not alone, however, for there was another side to the irony which Lloyd did not see. A sizable body of men loved the Democratic party and yet could not accept its nominee. That group was made up of gold Democrats who also had no faith in silver as a panacea; but in opposing silver they too accepted it as the paramount issue of the campaign.

The victory of silver forces in the Democratic convention was disturbing to gold Democrats, and like the Populists they were confused and divided. Looking to Grover Cleveland for guidance, they received little help. The President grumbled enough privately, but publicly he said nothing. Gold Democrats of the East tended to follow his example. Silver had won few converts in eastern states, and gold men still retained control over state Democratic organizations. If they sat tight, they seem to have believed, they could survive the silver craze. Their attitude was that of New Yorker David B. Hill, who told Charles S. Hamlin of Maine that "he was working hard for sound money" and would "not come out for Bryan." His only contribution to the campaign outside his own state was his famous quip: "I am still a Democrat—very still."

Out in the West, Bourbon Democrats found themselves in a different position. Silverites had taken over state organizations there, and after Bryan's nomination gold men had neither a state nor a national party to which they could turn. Thus the movement to establish an independent gold Democratic party originated in the Middle West. Former congressman William D. Bynum of Indiana promoted the idea, and it was in large part through his efforts that a conference of Bourbon Democrats was held in Chicago on July 23. The conference adopted a resolution calling for another Democratic convention. After a skeleton organization had been pieced together and after further conferences had been held, 824 gold Democrats convened at Indianapolis on September 2.

There was almost complete agreement on the platform, of course. The chief business of the National Democratic party, as the new organization had been termed, was the nomination of candidates. Very few men of national stature associated themselves with the party, so delegates had little choice but to name a comparative nonentity. The two chief contenders for the presidential nomination were General John M. Palmer, Senator from Illinois, and General Edward S. Bragg, a fighting campaigner from Wisconsin who had been the first to say of Cleveland, "We love him for the enemies he has made." The honor went to the seventy-nine year old Palmer, who had once before broken with the Democracy—back in 1854 when Senator Stephen A. Douglas tried to make support of the Kansas-Nebraska Act a test of party loyalty. Once a major-general in the Union Army, he had as his running mate Simon Bolivar Buckner, former governor of Kentucky, who had been a major-general in the Confederate Army.

Bryan, Weaver, Warner, and others looked upon the silver issue as one on which parties and leaders of reform could unite. But the silver issue cut across party lines; from one point of view it was more divisive than unifying. Teller and his followers had walked out of the GOP convention; Bynum and the Bourbons had formed a splinter Democratic party. The silver issue had wrought havoc in the Populist party. Even the Prohibition party split on the silver question. "Broad-gauge" prohibitionists who wanted to form an alliance with other reform groups, and who favored including a silver plank in their platform, broke with "narrow-gauge" prohibitionists who were interested mainly in doing away with strong drink.

Important as were party splits in and of themselves, the year 1896 was also important for what it had to teach about the operation of the American political system. After the tumult and the shouting of national conventions had died down, and the last hurrah for nominees had sounded, the choice presented to most voters had been effectively limited to a decision for or against silver. It was not as trivial and insignificant a choice as middle-road Populists and later historians thought it was. To be sure, Bryan's program was much narrower than the Omaha platform. Obviously a vote for or against silver was by no means a vote for or against the system of industrial capitalism which had developed in the United States. Bryan offered free silver as a remedy for chronic depression and unfair prices. It would correct, so he and his followers believed, a major flaw in what was potentially a successful economic system.

Some Americans, however, thought that system needed drastic overhauling and revision, not just tinkering. What were their choices in 1896? They could support the Socialist Labor candidate as did Henry Demarest Lloyd. Or they could vote for Bryan with the hope that further reforms would be developed after promised silver legislation had been passed and bimetallism established. The radical alternative which Populism—at least Lloyd's brand of Populism—seemed to promise had failed to materialize. It did not exist when voters went to the polls in November.

VIII

ON THE HUSTINGS

❁

ANY STUDY OF THE ELECTION OF 1896 MUST NECESsarily deal in contrasts. Radical Populists were impressed by the inequitable distribution of wealth which they associated with the development of industrial capitalism. They compared the advantages of the rich with the hardships of the poor, and they urged a program which they thought would establish social and economic justice. Farmers, losing steadily in market power, were growing increasingly conscious of disparities between prices of goods they bought and prices of goods they sold. Advocates of free coinage saw silver as a panacea that would bring the salvation of society and preserve the Republic. Men who stood by the gold standard regarded proposed silver legislation as dangerous. In their view it threatened the very structure of law and order on which society rested. Men of wealth worried about the chances of class conflict; some of them expected to hear at any time the opening shots of a revolution. Others, more aware of sectional than class differences, weighed the possibility of another civil war, pitting agricultural sections of the South and West against the industrial East.

The marked contrast between the campaign of McKinley and that of Bryan is only in part attributable to a difference of opinion on issues. Equally important were the means by which the two appealed for votes. In both cases, the activities of the candidate prior to the party convention provide a basis for understanding the more general canvass which followed. McKinley established an efficient organization long before his potential rivals within the GOP were ready to throw their hats into the ring. After his nomination that organization stood prepared to carry on to victory in November. Bryan paid little attention to organization prior to the Democratic convention. He directed his efforts toward propagating free silver ideas and creating a situation in which he would appear as the only logical choice of his party. It was essential to his plans that he avoid having any semblance of an organization. Thus at the start of the campaign McKinley appeared to have an advantage. But Republicans could ill afford to underestimate Bryan. He proposed to take his case to the voters, and few politicians have been so adept as he in pleading a case before the people.

At the beginning McKinley's managers had little idea of the demands which would be placed upon them during the summer of 1896. They anticipated the kind of electioneering that had become traditional in American politics, with Republicans hurling shafts at the luckless Cleveland administration from their customary protectionist position. Hanna, supremely confident, looked forward to a vacation cruise off the New England coast in August. But the Democratic convention in Chicago forced a change in plans. The campaign, observed Hanna after Bryan's nomination, "will be work and hard work from the start." With the nation still struggling to overcome economic stagnation, and with a spirit of unrest abroad in the land, the demand for silver might mean McKinley's defeat. The battle cry of "16 to 1" might well become a cry of victory.

Yet the McKinley-Hanna partnership had faced challenges before. Not for a moment did McKinley or any of the men close to him lose their heads. It was obvious that Bryan would win the states of the deep South and the far West. The Northeast seemed safe for McKinley, even though Tammany Hall did come out for Bryan late in

July. Thus the really crucial section was the Old Northwest. The five states of that region—Ohio, Indiana, Illinois, Michigan, and Wisconsin—held 88 electoral votes. Those, combined with the 117 from New England, New York, New Jersey, and Pennsylvania, would not give McKinley the victory in November, for he would still fall short of the 224 necessary votes. Nevertheless loss of any of the middle western states might well prove disastrous.

With such figures running through his mind, Hanna set up headquarters in Chicago. He left Dawes in charge there under the nominal supervision of Wisconsin's Henry C. Payne and traveled to New York to talk things over with William M. Osborne. When he arrived at the Waldorf, he was spotted by a group of reporters. "What will be the issue, Mr. Hanna?" queried one. "Our main issue," replied the astute campaign manager, "is to elect McKinley."

While New York offices were being organized, Hanna had other important matters to occupy his attention, among them an interview with Tom Platt. Platt knew when he had been beaten. He and Hanna shook hands, reported the *New York Times*, "in the most cordial manner, and they both declared that everything was harmonious and delightful between the Republican national organization and the Republican state organization." Eventually Matt Quay and Joseph Manley also came round to help out at headquarters.

Hanna worked harder at raising funds than he did at anything else. With a skill that amounted to genius he persuaded businessmen of both the worthiness of the cause and the necessity for large gifts. Not all of those who gave were Republicans. Democrat James J. Hill of the Great Northern believed so firmly in the gold standard that he helped Hanna canvass Wall Street. Gradually the war chest began to fill up. A gift of $250,000 from the Standard Oil Company proved that John D. Rockefeller knew where his best interests lay. New York Life came across with $50,000. The books of Charlie Dawes showed contributions from western railroads totaling $174,000. On September 11, Dawes noted in his diary that he had lunched with Hanna and that the campaign manager had handed him an envelope containing $50,000 in cash, the gift of one railroad.

The same day he deposited a check for a similar amount from another source. There were, of course, small checks too. But more than a fourth of the contributions coming into the Chicago office were in amounts of $1,000 or more.

Estimates on the total amount received and spent have varied widely. Dawes calculated that something over $3,570,000 was collected. The figure is doubtless reliable, though it does not include services such as transportation and the use of telegraphic facilities. The best estimates of expenditures cluster around the $3,500,000 figure, and they are usually coupled with the observation that Dawes and Hanna permitted no waste and that each dollar carried its share of the load. Nevertheless Republican expenditures were twice as great as they had been in 1892. Nothing provides a better indication of how seriously McKinley and his aides took the campaign.

Democrats sometimes charged that Hanna was operating a slush fund on an unprecedented scale and that he was buying up votes in callous disregard for democratic processes. While he may have been willing to spend money in this way—Hanna was a pragmatist for whom ends justified means—there is little evidence to substantiate the charge. Boodle has a way of adding up, and as any clever politician knows, it is in the long run a very costly and ineffective method of securing votes. McKinley had better ways to spend the funds at his disposal.

He and his advisers allocated a generous portion of the Republican budget to what McKinley and Hanna called a campaign of education. Rallies and speeches were valued not merely because they stirred up enthusiasm for the GOP; they were highly regarded and frequently subsidized because they indoctrinated voters on intricacies of public finance in general and the money question in particular. The Speakers Bureau in Chicago made engagements for some 1,400 speakers. Yet Republican strategists believed the written word just as important as the spoken word. "There is an intense feeling everywhere, and much interest in this money question," Osborne wrote McKinley in mid-August, "and we have got to furnish the literature that will enlighten the people." Perry Heath of the Cincinnati *Commercial Gazette* headed the Bureau of Publication and Printing, and his department was an active one. A month after Osborne posted his letter, Heath reported to Dawes that he had distributed a hundred million pieces of literature. By the end of the campaign at least two hundred million leaflets and pamphlets had been sent out. There were more than 275 different items among them, and some had been translated into German, French, Spanish, Italian, Swedish, Norwegian, Finnish, Dutch, and Hebrew. In addition, Republicans printed scores of broadsides, posters, cartoons, and inscriptions. *The Review of Reviews* observed that the number of documents sent out in 1896 exceeded by more than 50 per cent the number of documents issued by the Republican National Committee since the founding of the party.

This was not all. Republicans enjoyed overwhelming newspaper support, and they made the most of it. Three and a half columns of specially prepared matter were sent out every week to a preferred list of country newspapers with an aggregate weekly circulation of 1,650,000. Another group of papers with a total weekly circulation of about one million received plate matter. Hundreds of other newspapers were supplied with ready prints, statements, and other materials. According to one estimate, every week at least five million families read newspapers which used the matter sent out by the Bureau of Publication and Printing.

The activities of the McKinley organization made the efforts of the Democratic National Committee look like a peanut operation. As a matter of fact the Committee was not even appointed until the second week in August. National Chairman James K. Jones made tentative arrangements for offices in Washington and Chicago before going to the Populist convention as an interested observer. He also visited Bryan in Lincoln and discussed the campaign. But the establishment of an organization was deferred until after Bryan's acceptance speech in New York. On August 3, William P. St. John, in his dual role as National Treasurer of both the Democratic and Silver parties, opened his headquarters in New York City. He put up pictures of Bryan and Sewall, but not much more was done until Bryan appeared a week later.

Finally Chairman Jones announced the appointment of a National Committee and the establishment of headquarters in Chicago and Washington. The Silver party and the Populist party both had Washington offices, and Democrats hoped that the important work of coordinating activities could be carried on there. St. John remained in New York, however, contributing his bit to Democratic inefficiency by keeping out of immediate touch with national headquarters.

The Democratic National Committee attempted, in a limited way, to duplicate the activities of the McKinley organization. It established a speakers bureau in Chicago, and some campaign literature was sent out from there. The National Silver party distributed, in English and German editions, a million copies of a pamphlet by the Most Reverend William John Walsh, Archbishop of Dublin, who suggested a relationship between hard money and Irish land problems. Some 125,000 copies of *Coin's Financial School* were also sent out. The headquarters of all parties supporting Bryan organized Bryan clubs and silver clubs.

Yet the most conscientious labors of silver men, Democrats, and Populists were no match for what was being done by Republicans. Even if St. John's office had been more efficiently coordinated with Bryan's headquarters, there would have been difficulties. As it was, campaign workers found themselves constantly embarrassed for lack of funds. On August 22, Chairman Jones wrote an open letter to the American people pleading for contributions. It was on the plain folks of the United States, he said, that the Bryan campaign must depend: "No matter in how small sums, no matter by what humble contributions, let the friends of liberty and national honor contribute all they can to the good cause." The pathetic appeal brought in a little, but not as much as Jones had hoped. The best fund raiser among Bryan's followers was William Randolph Hearst. Through the New York *Journal* he offered to match contributions dollar for dollar. He eventually turned over $40,901.20 to the National Committee. It was the largest gift Bryan received, but by Republican standards it was obviously a paltry sum.

Hearst's services were unusual in one other respect. His *Journal* was the only major Democratic newspaper in New York to lend its support to Bryan. The *Sun*, the *Herald*, the *World*, the *Evening Post*, and the Brooklyn *Eagle* all favored maintaining the gold standard. Those papers, however, only did what the largest newspapers all over the country were doing. In New England the Boston *Herald*, the *Globe*, the *Post*, the Springfield *Republican*, and the Providence *Journal* also opposed Bryan's election. The Chicago *Chronicle* aligned itself with gold, depriving the Democrats of a major paper in the Windy City. In Baltimore the *Sun* and the *News* rejected silver as did the *Record* and *Times* in Philadelphia. Some of the most important papers in the South, the Louisville *Courier-Journal*, the New Orleans *Picayune*, the Charleston *News and Courier*, and the Richmond *Times*, declined to support the Democratic ticket. Never had the shift in newspaper sentiment been so widespread.

Clearly Bryan and his managers could never hope to compete with the McKinley-Hanna partnership in organization, in finances, or in campaign literature. Democrats faced a further disadvantage in that factory owners and managers overwhelmingly favored McKinley. Bryan and his supporters always claimed that workers were coerced into voting Republican in 1896. Although there may not have been as much coercion as Democrats charged, shop owners did set up McKinley placards, speakers did talk to men during the lunch hour, leaflets advancing the case for gold were distributed with pay envelopes, notices threatening lay-offs if Bryan won were posted, and railroads did cooperate in organizing excursions to Canton.

With much of this McKinley and Hanna had little to do. How factory managers chose to support the Republican party was their own concern. When Democrats charged that manufacturers were pressuring workingmen, however, the Republicans responded with charges of their own. Silver mine owners, they contended, were financing Bryan's entire campaign. Nothing could have been more obvious than that mine owners stood to gain by free silver legislation. Yet while Democrats would certainly have accepted money from that source, it was not forthcoming in the amounts McKinley men would have had the voters believe. Even if it had been, it still would not have come close to equaling contributions made to the GOP.

Every campaign has its unpleasant side. As usual, the American Protective Association busied itself with rumormongering, and loose talk influenced some votes. Precisely what effect the A.P.A. may have had is difficult to determine, however, for its members were as vague in their allegations as they were divided on whom to support. Perhaps charges and countercharges of party leaders and others tended to cancel out in 1896, although the evidence seems to suggest that Democrats had more reason to complain than had Republicans. However that may be, Bryan gained little from the whispering campaign or from the controversy over financial backing. In fact, one might be tempted to ask at this point if he had anything at all going for him. The answer, of course, is that he did. He had his youth, his vigor, his personal magnetism, his passionate belief in the cause of silver, and above all his oratorical power.

Bryan men who had watched him rise from obscurity to fame and who had seen how he captivated audiences were optimistic. "He will set the prairies of the west and south on fire with a wave of enthusiasm that will sweep far toward the east," enthused the *Illinois State Register* of Springfield. At the Chicago convention a southern delegate had given Bryan a rabbit's foot. Shortly after his nomination he received another from Helena, Montana. According to the accompanying message, the charm had been touched to the Nebraskan's name as telegraphic reports of the balloting had come in, "as a result of which . . . there was continued gain in your favor." Well-wishers may not have been in a position to donate money, but they did contribute rabbits' feet, and before long Bryan acquired a sizable collection. He would need all the luck they might bring.

Luck would not be decisive, however, and the champion of free silver knew it. His analysis of the forces at work in the campaign bore a marked similarity to Mark Hanna's analysis. Anyone who examined electoral votes and who kept abreast of current events could see that the crucial states were those east of the Missouri River and north of the Ohio. If Bryan could hold his own in that area, and perhaps pick up some support in the East, he could emerge the victor in November. How might he get his message across? There was only one way to do it. Without adequate funds, without a highly trained or well-coordinated organization, without newspaper support, Bryan would have to go to the people. He would have to meet them face to face on their home grounds.

Counting his journey to the Chicago convention, Bryan made four campaign trips which took him from Nebraska and the Dakotas to the Atlantic Coast, and from Tennessee and North Carolina to Maine and Minnesota. He covered the states of the Old Northwest as completely as was humanly possible—indeed his labors struck contemporaries as superhuman—and he carried the silver banner into the very shadows of Wall Street. His campaign began in earnest on the afternoon of August 8, when he and Mrs. Bryan prepared to board the train for Chicago. They were on their way to New York, where the candidate would make his acceptance speech in Madison Square Garden on the eleventh. To the crowd which had gathered at the Lincoln depot to see them off, Bryan explained the reasons for the trip. "I expressed the desire to be notified in New York," he said, "in order that our cause might be presented first in the heart of what now seems to be the enemy's country, but which we hope to be our country before this campaign is over." Later, at a rally in Pittsburgh, he promised "that in the progress of this campaign not a single private in the ranks will stand nearer to the enemy's lines than him in whose hand is the standard."

Bryan was assuming the offensive, and he hoped that his speech in Madison Square Garden would give him a victory in the first engagement of the conflict of 1896. He had decided to read his address, and in writing it out he had labored long and hard to express as cogently as possible the arguments for silver. It was not, however, the tour de force he hoped it might be. At least it did not leave the gold men demoralized and disconsolate. The eleventh was one of those blistering hot days that sometimes make New York a steaming concrete jungle. The air in the Garden was stifling, and Governor Stone was both dull and long-winded in his notification speech. Hundreds who had come out of idle curiosity quit the premises long before Bryan had finished speaking. The number of those who left was exaggerated by the eastern press, but the fact that some did leave provided an excuse to characterize the meeting as a complete failure.

It was not a failure. A reporter for *The Review of Reviews* thought Bryan's audience "immensely enthusiastic," and he took pains to point out that "the vast bulk of the crowd remained to hear the very last word of the speech." For people to sit in such heat through two hours of a speech they could read in the papers the next day was a real compliment. But a hostile press did not report it that way, and Bryan's "failure" in Madison Square Garden became one of the legends of the campaign. The candidate himself was certainly not disappointed, and he was amused rather than disturbed by the newspaper accounts. With a feeling of satisfaction he and his wife left the city to spend a few days with friends in Upper Red Hook, where Bryan rested and worked on his letter of acceptance. The couple then returned to Lincoln via Buffalo, Cleveland, Columbus, Toledo, Chicago, and Milwaukee. Representatives of the Silver party had gathered in Lincoln to meet them, and Bryan gave another major address in accepting the silver nomination.

"It is now just about one month since I left Nebraska and turned eastward," he told his supporters. "It has been an interesting trip. I want to assure you that the sentiment in favor of the free coinage of silver is a growing sentiment." All along the way crowds had gathered at railroad stations, and Bryan had spoken to them about what was on his heart and mind. His voice, powerful as it was, almost gave out at times. Despite the heat wave—for several days newspapers reported deaths from prostration—people turned out to hear him. On the return trip crowds were so large at Columbus, Toledo, and South Bend that no building could accommodate them, and rallies were held in open fields. The candidate had every reason to believe that silver sentiment was growing.

After three days at home Bryan was off again to face more crowds, make more speeches, and shake more hands. This time he left Mrs. Bryan in Lincoln, although she met him later for the last leg of his 13,000-mile journey. His movements attracted attention, and reporters were always on hand to send in stories about what he said. Heading first south and then east, Bryan traveled through Kansas City, St. Louis, Kentucky, and Tennessee to Greensboro, North Carolina. There he turned northward, stopping at Washington and continuing on through New York and up into New England. After addressing a crowd of some 75,000 in Boston and visiting with Arthur Sewall in Maine, he returned to the Middle West. During the month of October he campaigned vigorously in the border states and in Indiana, Ohio, Illinois, Minnesota, and Michigan. Before returning to Nebraska, Bryan spoke to huge rallies in Chicago. His fourth and final trip was a short one; he wound up his campaign with a junket through his home state.

By the time election day finally arrived, Bryan had traveled 18,009 miles according to his reckoning. He had delivered some 600 speeches to perhaps five million people in twenty-seven states. During much of his travels Bryan had made his own arrangements, buying his train tickets, riding on regular coaches, sometimes even carrying his own luggage. Not until October did the National Committee provide him with a private car, "The Idler," a name Bryan was justified in thinking singularly inappropriate.

Why did he do it? Why did he put up with the inconvenience, risking his voice and his health? Bryan gave a partial answer when he addressed that huge throng in Boston. "While our opponents are spreading literature by the ton, the people are joining in the crusade for the restoration of bimetallism," he said. "We have no great campaign fund with which to supply those who want to read with all the literature they would like to have."

But the best answer came on October 28, when the Democratic clubs and labor organizations of Chicago staged a reception at Battery D. Jewish Democrats presented Bryan with a badge, and in acknowledging the gift he said, "Our opponents have sometimes tried to make it appear that we were attacking a race when we denounced the financial policy of the Rothschilds. But we are not; we are as much opposed to the financial policy of J. Pierpont Morgan as we are to the financial policy of the Rothschilds. We are not attacking a race; we are attacking greed and avarice, which know neither race nor religion." Earlier in the ceremonies someone had referred to the fight between David and Goliath. "David conquered," Bryan pointed out, "not because he was stronger, but because he was on the right side; and if in this contest I am likened to David, let me reply that as David triumphed because he was right, so my only hope of victory is in the righteousness of my cause." A good Jeffersonian, Bryan was "willing to trust to the intelligence of the American people to decide whether this Government is safer in the hands of those who believe in the ability of the people to govern themselves, or in the hands of the trusts and syndicates which have been bleeding the people." The people would rule. It was to them that Bryan went with his condemnation of greed and avarice. It was to them that he went with his appeal for a cause in which he believed.

How successful was the David of the silver forces? Hoosier politician George W. Julian had fought through many a hard campaign. One of the founders of the Republican party, he had been associated first with its radical wing in the sixties and then with its liberal wing in the seventies. Now in 1896 he supported the Palmer-Buckner ticket. "The political canvass has been a perfect surprise to the people of all parties," he wrote in his diary late in October. The Democratic candidate seemed to be winning new converts every day, and the enthusiasm of his followers seemed to be increasing. Julian could not understand Bryan; he was puzzled about the sources of his strength. "If he can succeed with all the business interests of the country against him, solidly, and nearly all the newspapers, and all the colleges and educational influences, it can only be accounted for on the theory of a stupendous retrogression in the work of civilization, which would be at war with the philosophy of evolution and irreconcilable with the belief in a divine Providence."

Bryan's success was such that McKinley and Hanna could not rely on evolutionary processes any more than they could rely solely on efficiency in organization, fund-collecting, and propaganda distribution. McKinley too believed in meeting the people face to face, but not so much because he thought them competent judges. He wanted to meet people because he wanted to reassure them. The advance agent of prosperity wanted to quiet their depression-born anxieties. He wanted to be certain they were with him. He would not go to them, for that would be undignified and unbecoming in a presidential candidate. It was also unnecessary. With apparently unlimited resources and with the cooperation of railroads, the people could be brought to him. A vital part of the McKinley campaign was the way in which a confrontation of candidate and voters was arranged.

Characteristically, nothing was left to chance. Some delegations to Canton were set up by McKinley's workers in the field; others came on their own initiative. Either way, there was always an exchange of letters or a preliminary conference before a party put in its appearance. McKinley always wanted to know what its leaders intended to say, and if the speech of a visiting dignitary did not strike just the right note changes were requested. When the train bearing a delegation puffed into the Canton station, it was met by at least one band and sometimes several of them. It was escorted up the Market Street hill to the modest house where the McKinleys lived. Then there were refreshments and well-rehearsed speeches. Although the Major knew exactly what visiting luminaries would say, he always managed to appear interested. He arranged his Napoleonic features into a look of rapt attention that seemed to suggest both modesty and dignity as speakers extolled his virtues. He always replied with a few well-chosen remarks, taking great care to display his familiarity with the peculiar problems of the area whence the delegation had come. There was a round of handshaking as the group took its leave to go back and tell the home folks all about it.

The front porch campaign had many advantages. While it was almost impossible in the quiet Ohio town to generate the spontaneous enthusiasm that characterized some Democratic rallies, there were no slips of the tongue. To meet delegations of the size and number that came was arduous. On September 18, according to the *New York Times,* some 80,000 people visited Canton. On October 4, McKinley met thirty delegations and made fourteen formal speeches. On the eighteenth he saw 36,000 people from Pennsylvania, Michigan, and Ohio. The candidate did not lounge around on his front porch; he worked hard throughout the summer and early fall. But one of the chief advantages to his technique was that it spared him the strains and tensions to which the peripatetic Bryan was subjected. And he no doubt reached as many voters, at least indirectly, for every person who made the pilgrimage to see the great man told others about the experience.

What sort of message did McKinley give his supporters to take back to their friends and neighbors? Although the adoption of a gold plank by the Republicans in St. Louis had attracted great attention, he hoped at first to emphasize the tariff during the campaign. He felt at ease in discussing the tariff issue. He thought he understood it as well as anybody did, and he sincerely believed that the Wilson-Gorman tariff had helped to bring on economic stagnation. Furthermore, his own position on the tariff, unlike his position on the silver question, had always been consistent. He had never vacillated from his protectionist views. Bryan's nomination on a silver platform and his reluctance to discuss anything but silver, however, forced a change in the content of McKinley's speeches.

The line that Bryan took throughout the campaign was best enunciated in his Madison Square Garden address, and the speech therefore merits careful consideration, even though he said nothing that he had not said many times before. He began by taking up the charge that he and his supporters "not only meditate an attack upon the rights of property, but are the foes both of social order and national honor." It was not true. Bryan yielded to no one in his devotion to the doctrine set forth by Andrew Jackson: "In the full enjoyment of the gifts of Heaven and the fruits of superior industry, economy, and virtue, every man is equally entitled to protection by law." But Bryan emphasized the importance of equal protection; like Jackson he opposed privilege and favoritism. "No government is worthy of the name which is not able to protect from every arm uplifted for his injury the humblest citizen who lives beneath the flag." And it followed that injurious legislation would have to be remedied by those who suffered rather than by those who enjoyed its benefits. The cause of silver was the cause of the people.

Bryan questioned the sincerity of those who called for bimetallism through international agreement. Honest money could not be expected at the hands of those who deal dishonestly with the people. What was the test of honesty in money? "An absolutely honest dollar would not vary in its general purchasing power; it would be absolutely stable when measured by average prices." Neither monometallism nor bimetallism provided "an absolutely just standard of value." Yet bimetallism was better "because it makes a nearer approach to stability, to honesty, to justice, than a gold standard possibly can." Farmers opposed the gold standard. It had brought about a price decline in agricultural commodities. But at the same time the farmers' taxes had not been decreased, their debts had not fallen, and the railroad rates they had to pay had not been reduced. Wage earners also opposed the gold standard. They knew that while it raised purchasing power it made the dollar more difficult to obtain. It made employment less permanent and loss of work more probable. Since professional classes, merchants, investors, and manufacturers in the long run derived their support from laborers and farmers, it was clear that all classes of society had an interest—or should have had an interest—in restoring bimetallism.

The silver-tongued orator admitted that a few persons profited by a gold standard. Those whose income was fixed for life, whose income did not depend on business conditions, would obviously benefit from an appreciating dollar. But even the holders of fixed investments could see that the gold standard threatened the general welfare. Stability was the object to be achieved. A river fed from two sources would always be more uniform in volume than one fed from only one source. "So in the case of bimetallism; the volume of metallic money receives contributions from both the gold mines and the silver mines, and therefore varies less, and the dollar resting upon two metals is less changeable in its purchasing power than the dollar which rests upon one metal only."

Bryan did not question the natural laws of economics. The best known was supply and demand, and upon that law Democrats built their case. "We apply this law to money when we say that a reduction in the volume of money will raise the purchasing power of the dollar; we also apply the law of supply and demand to silver when we say that a new demand for silver created by law will raise the price of silver bullion." Here was the answer to "the most persistent misrepresentation that we have to meet," the charge that the Chicago platform called for "the payment of debts in fifty-cent dollars." When a mint price for silver had been once more established, there would be no glutted silver market to bring down the price of bullion. "Under bimetallism silver bullion will be worth as much as silver coin, just as gold bullion is now worth as much as gold coin, and we believe that a silver dollar will be worth as much as a gold dollar." There would be no fifty cent dollars.

Bryan has often been criticized for placing so much emphasis on silver in 1896. Upon occasion he did touch on other matters. In his letter of acceptance he developed in some detail his Jeffersonian view of democracy. He also spoke out against the bond policy of the Cleveland administration and the use of injunctions in labor disputes. He suggested legislation to set up some means of arbitration in conflicts between labor and management. He favored an income tax, the regulation of trusts through the Interstate Commerce Commission, and limiting the terms of appointive offices. The Democratic platform was by no means a narrow one, yet Bryan left no doubt that he considered silver the paramount issue. He steadfastly refused to discuss the tariff. "Whatever may be the individual views of citizens as to the relative merits of protection and tariff reform," he wrote in his letter of acceptance, "all must recognize that, until the money question is fully and finally settled, the American people will not consent to the consideration of any other important question."

William McKinley was at first disappointed in the turn which the great debate of 1896 had taken. Had the silver question been left out of it, he could easily have pinned the blame for depression on the Democrats by showing that their low tariff had brought it about. Yet he soon came to realize that Bryan's emphasis on silver provided him with opportunities for effective counterthrusts without really eliminating the tariff as a subject for discussion. Before long, Republican speakers were following McKinley's example in coupling free silver and free trade as vagaries peculiar to the Democracy and dangerous to the Republic.

The McKinley-Hanna partnership found several effective ways of meeting silver arguments. In appealing to farmers they contended that the real cause of low prices was domestic overproduction and foreign competition. The gold standard had not brought about the farmers' dilemma, and the adoption of free coinage would not help them. Fortunately for the GOP, reports of wheat shortages in India, Russia, and Australia had the effect of stimulating wheat prices during September and October. The price rise was caused as much by speculation as it was by a decline in supply, but Republican newspapers and speakers seized upon it as proof of their argument that overproduction meant low farm prices. They followed this up, of course, by contending that a protective tariff would restore not only industrial prosperity but prosperity in agriculture as well. "Depression in agriculture always follows low tariff legislation," McKinley told a delegation of farmers. "The farmer is suffering today because the number of his competitors has increased and his best customers are out of work." Not much could be done about competition except by a tariff that would set factories to operating again. "You don't get customers through the mint," concluded McKinley, "you get them through the factory."

The arguments which McKinley developed had appeal for workers too. "I believe the business of this free Government is to preserve the American market to the American producer, whether in the factory or the farm, and to preserve the American mines and the factories of the American workmen," he told a delegation of miners from West Newton, Pennsylvania. What was needed was a restoration of confidence. "We do not want any cheap money, any more than we want cheap labor in the United States." McKinley continued to work away at the theme that silver meant a fifty cent dollar despite Bryan's attempt to destroy the effectiveness of the argument. "When the miners of West Newton have dug their coal by their honest toil," said the Major, who knew from long experience how to talk to workers, "they want to be paid in dollars that are equal to the best dollars of the world and will not depreciate in the future, and will be as good on one day and in one country as in another."

With the silver question assuming such significance in the pleas of both Republicans and Democrats, it would have been surprising if there had been no special "campaign coins" minted. As a matter of fact large quantities of funny money circulated during the campaign. Republicans found it a device for illustrating their contention that silver would create cheaper dollars. One campaign coin was inscribed on its obverse side, FREE COINAGE, 16 TO 1; the reverse carried the notation, FROM SILVER MINES OF BUNCO STATE. Much more clever, however, was a coin which bore a caricature bust of Bryan with the inscription, IN GOD WE TRUST . . . FOR THE OTHER 47 CENTS.

Bryan himself appeared to enjoy such nonsense as much as anybody; the man's patience and good humor seemed almost unbounded. Those who worked with him knew that he could be unyielding to a point where he exasperated everyone, but he seldom lost his temper even under the most trying circumstances. At New

Haven, Connecticut, for example, a large number of Yale students joined the crowd with the evident intention of creating a disturbance. When Bryan tried to speak, he was constantly interrupted by catcalls, organized cheers, and raucous songs. Finally a band appeared, and Bryan excused himself from making any further remarks. Democrats scored the students for their ungentlemanly behavior. Professor Henry B. Wright, acting president of the University, regretted the incident, but pointed out that boys would be boys. Bryan agreed. "Having been a college boy myself," he said in a later speech, "I attribute their interruption more to youthful exuberance than to any intention to interfere with free speech."

There were occasions, however, when Bryan's ire was aroused. Josephus Daniels, who accompanied him to New York in September, later recalled that the candidate "may not have been mad, but he was 'hell-fired' vexed when he got to Wilmington, Delaware." Bryan was reading the New York newspapers which had been put on board the train at Dover. Suddenly he thrust a paper in Daniels' face, and pointing a thick finger at the headlines he barked, "Read that!" It was a report that John Boyd Thatcher, who had been nominated for governor by New York Democrats, had announced his refusal to support the silver plank of the Chicago platform. Bryan was incensed, especially so since the same convention that nominated Thatcher had approved the entire platform. The action Bryan took was entirely in character; he could excuse personal insults, but never disloyalty to the cause he thought so important. He refused to enter New York until he had assurances that Thatcher would turn down the nomination. When he received those assurances, he went to New York and spoke there. Thatcher, to complete arrangements, refused to become a candidate for governor of the state.

Unquestionably the most nagging vexation of the campaign from Bryan's point of view was the problem posed by the Populists. Senator Butler, who replaced Taubeneck as National Chairman, did as much as he could to coordinate Populist activities with those of the Democrats. In September he and Jones agreed on a plan to secure fusion through the various state organizations. Eventually, largely through Butler's good offices, fusion tickets apportioning Bryan-Sewall and Bryan-Watson electors were arranged in twenty-eight states.

It was, however, a difficult task, particularly in the South. Neither southern Populists nor southern Democrats could work up much enthusiasm for fusion. Only six southern and near-southern states (Arkansas, Kentucky, Louisiana, Missouri, North Carolina, and West Virginia) accepted arrangements which Jones and Butler sought to work out. "There has been so much lethargy and friction among our people over the Vice Presidential muddle," wrote Butler to Ignatius Donnelly, "and besides, so much local friction, due to antagonism that has resulted in the past between Populists and Democrats, that I fear very much for the result. . . ." For his part, Senator Jones thought southern Populists "not a creditable class." He predicted that they would do all they could to create confusion. "They will go with the negroes, where they belong," he added slurringly.

Tom Watson was a real thorn in the flesh of fusionists. Defying Democratic domination, he refused to behave. He campaigned in the West, and everywhere he went he preached middle-of-the-road Populism. He urged his audiences to vote for Bryan, but not once did he have a good word to say for fusion. "Why should the Democratic managers demand of us a complete and unconditional surrender?" he asked. "They say we must fuse, but their idea of fusion is that we play minnow while they play trout; we play June bug while they play duck; we play Jonah while they play whale. . . ." He thought Butler a traitor for attempting to cooperate with such men.

To Democrats—and to Butler—Watson seemed willful and intransigent. They did not appear to understand that he was fighting to save his party and that forcing the withdrawal of Sewall was his only hope. After the St. Louis convention Butler had announced that Populists would not swallow the Democratic vice-presidential candidate, yet he postponed making any demand that Sewall withdraw. Not until after several fusion agreements had been reached did he make the demand; by then it was an empty formality.

Butler's delay in notifying Watson of his nomination proved equally frustrating. Watson had to insist publicly that the Populist Notification Committee act. At last on September 14, Butler sent letters of notification to both Bryan and Watson. They were phrased so as to cause Bryan the least possible embarrassment; the People's party exacted no promises of him, and he accepted "without departing from the platform adopted by the Democratic National Convention in Chicago." Watson was furious and he said as much in his reply, but the letter was not released until after the election.

Several years later Bryan admitted that the Democrats had treated Watson shabbily. At the time, however, Bryan believed that he was making the best of a bad situation. Even though running with both Sewall and Watson was difficult, Bryan thought it preferable to having either one of them withdraw. Populists could take some comfort in the thought that by having their own vice-presidential candidate they might preserve their party. Furthermore, Bryan's willingness to put up with Watson no doubt helped the Nebraskan to establish friendly relations with other Populists. Ignatius Donnelly, disappointed as he was with results of the conventions, nevertheless worked hard for Bryan. He went to Lincoln early in September, and he was among those who greeted the candidate on his return from New York. "He is a very able, shrewd, wise man," Donnelly wrote in his diary. "He was very kind & complimentary—said Weaver and myself were the only two Populists he could depend upon, etc." Then the old war horse of Minnesota politics added, "I have a dim hope that I may perchance get a seat in his cabinet if he is elected—but I have been disappointed so often that I am not sanguine as to any thing." Still it appeared to him that Bryan had been "raised up by Providence to save the country from sinking into old world conditions."

Whether Populists adjusted gracefully to the peculiar conditions of 1896 as Donnelly seemed to, or whether they railed against fate as did Tom Watson, there could be little doubt that their party was dying. Such has usually been the lot of third parties in the United States. But the Populists should not be compared with the National Silver party and the National Democratic party which were actually nothing more than temporary expedients, parties in name only. Both of them, to use the analogy later employed by a silver orator, could be likened to a mule which "has no ancestry and no hope of posterity." Although Senator Teller and other Silver party members were active in the campaign and contributed significantly to Bryan's cause, the party as an organization played only a minor role. The gold Democratic candidates—the only ones in the race who defended the Cleveland administration—were actually something of a joke. "You would laugh yourself sick could you see old Palmer," wrote Judge Kenesaw M. Landis to Daniel Lamont, Cleveland's Secretary of War. "He has actually gotten it into his head he is running for office." Landis misrepresented the facts, of course, for Palmer frequently advised voters to cast their ballots for McKinley. The splinter parties could not be ignored, however; while they were not likely to poll many votes, those they did obtain could be decisive. Time would tell.

Throughout the canvass McKinley made much of the divisions among his opponents. "We have but one political party which is united, and that is ours," he told a delegation of farmers from Somerset, Pennsylvania. "Discord reigns in all others." Harmony and prosperity, sound economic policy and patriotism—those were the things McKinley stood for. He wound up his campaign on Saturday, October 31, with an immense rally in Canton. Foraker was there and spoke brilliantly. Some two score bands kept the air ringing with stirring marches. Hanna had earlier suggested that everyone fly the flag on that day, and as far as the eye could see, flags fluttered in the fall breeze. "Glorious old banner it is," said McKinley in concluding his campaign. "So long as we carry it in our hands and have what it typifies in our hearts, the Republic and our splendid free institutions will be forever secure."

While the Republican candidate was identifying himself with the

Red White and Blue, Bryan was telling a crowd in Ottumwa, Iowa, that "our appeal has been to the great producing masses and to those who believe that the prosperity of the nation must begin with those who toil and find its way upward through the other classes of society." Once more he affirmed his faith in silver. "My hand has been used until it is sore, but it can handle a pen to sign a free-coinage bill, if I am elected. I have been wearied with work, but I still have the physical strength to stand between the people, if they elect me, and the Wall street syndicates which have been bleeding this country." Back in 1893, when Congressman Bryan had spoken against repeal of the Sherman Silver Purchase Act, he had asked the Democratic party if it would rise to greet a new dawn or if it would turn its face to the setting sun. "Will it choose blessings or cursings—life or death—which? Which?" The party had clearly given its response. Now Bryan was asking the American people for an answer to the same question.

IX

NOVEMBER 3, AND AFTER

ON TUESDAY, NOVEMBER 3, 1896, CITIZENS SOLEMNLY cast their votes to give William McKinley a decisive victory over William Jennings Bryan. Across the country, from Maine to California, they went to the polls early. Despite a record turnout the day passed quietly. "There has not been a hand raised for trouble and not an arrest made for disorderly conduct in the city limits," reported the Chicago Chief of Police. "The few saloon-keepers who opened their doors were arrested quickly. It is a unique record in the history of the city. . . ." The Pittsburgh *Post* observed little business being transacted: "the streets were only sprinkled with people, and altogether a sort of Sunday air pervaded the old city and the Northside." Des Moines, noted the *Iowa State Register,* "never before witnessed an election in which the voters were got out with so little effort." Carriages hired by committees of both parties to take people to voting places stood idle in the late afternoon, "for in almost every precinct the number of voters almost equalled the number registered before half the afternoon was over."

Everywhere it was the same. Even though the day was unusually calm, the Minneapolis *Tribune* thought the election one of the most exciting ever known in Minnesota, "the interest being deep and silent." Never before in the history of Council Bluffs, Iowa, had so large a proportion of the vote been cast before noon. The *Rocky Mountain News* found the people of Denver "were in earnest on the issues, and voted their convictions without discussion or interference." Out in San Francisco, everything passed off smoothly, and "only two arrests for illegal voting were made."

The citizens of Canton, Ohio, rose early to make the most of a day that would put their town indelibly on the map. The calm that prevailed across the country was broken here; men were marching and bands were playing at six o'clock in the morning. Before nine, Major McKinley appeared on his front porch from which he had greeted so many delegations and made so many speeches. He inspected the body of horsemen known as the McKinley Troop; it had done escort duty during the campaign, but the Major had declined its services for the day. He thought he should vote "as unobtrusively as any private citizen." Passing to the street, he walked with his brother Abner and his wife's cousin, Sam Saxton, to the voting place. There was a line there, and the Major quietly took his place behind a mechanic in working clothes. His face took on a serious expression as he went inside the little building. After a few minutes he emerged from behind the cheap calico curtain of the booth, bowed to judges and spectators, and returned to the street without so much as a flicker of a smile. "This is a solemn occasion for me," he said to a friend. "I am deeply impressed by it."

In the meantime, William Jennings Bryan had spent Monday night in Omaha speaking to cheering crowds in a last minute appeal. He arose refreshed at 6:30 and ate one of the gargantuan breakfasts that had inspired much comment during the campaign. He downed a large beefsteak, an omelette, a dish of potatoes, and two cups of coffee before driving to the train with Mrs. Bryan and Governor Holcomb. At the Lincoln depot he was met by a brass band and an enthusiastic crowd which led him to the fire engine house that served as a polling place in his precinct. There, in a dark room where tethered horses were standing, he marked his ballot by the light of a lantern. While he was waiting to hand it in, wrote reporter James Creelman, "the newspaper correspondents leaning against the ropes went through a funny pantomime, as if they were trying to influence the leader's vote, and he went through mock gestures of resistance to temptation, shaking his head and rolling his eyes reproachfully at the writers who had accompanied him in his wonderful 18,000 mile journey." Finally he stepped to the box, looking as "Savonarola might have looked when he defied Rome." There was a blinding glare and a cloud of smoke as a photographer's assistant set off a shovel of flash powder. Bryan walked out to the street, the band struck up a lively march, and the spirited procession escorted him home.

It was, indeed, a day to remember. As the hours passed, emotions began to mount. When dusk settled over cities and towns, and men came home from work, people began to gather in the streets. Crowds collected in front of newspaper offices where arrangements had been made to post returns. The more affluent papers in the cities had erected huge canvas screens on which figures were flashed by means of stereopticon projectors. In Chicago 25,000 people gathered in the Coliseum, where Bryan had been nominated, to watch a special election night show sponsored by the Chicago *Tribune.*

It was a night to remember too. "Who has not seen an election crowd, and yet who can properly describe one?" queried a reporter of the Philadelphia *North American.* Nevertheless he made the attempt. He found many types among the hundred thousand people surging up and down the main avenues of Philadelphia. There was, first of all, the "steady, sober business man, anxious to see whether his business was to be jeopardized by the election of a repudiationist, or whether the good sense of the country had overcome such an idea and returned Major McKinley by a rousing majority." He stood apart, as much as that was possible, from the pushing throng. Not so "the callow youth" who "sported a big yellow or white chrysanthemum" depending upon whether he supported silver or gold. "He carried in his hand a big horn, and blew it at such frequent intervals that all of his neighbors in the crowd wished that they might be transported for the nonce to some foreign isle."

The noisy young man was "the cynosure of all eyes, and of none so prominently as those of the many pretty girls who were abroad." There were blondes, brunettes, short girls, tall girls, girls who were "neither 'high nor low,' but [were] ready for every 'Jack' that came along, and who [were] ready to be made 'game' of." There were loving couples too. And of course there was "the masher, who thought that he looked too sweet for anything and who was constantly winking at every maiden that passed him." Small boys were everywhere, getting into everybody's way and sometimes into trouble with one of the three hundred "minions of the law" posted on Chestnut Street. Finally there were the busiest men in all that vast multitude, the hawkers who sold false moustaches, buttons, badges, chrysanthemums, flags, and other "trifles light as air."

So it was in every city in the land. The strain of waiting was over; tensions of the day which had been so peaceful on the surface snapped as hurrah after hurrah rang out in the night air. A reporter standing on the tenth floor of the Carnegie Building in Pittsburgh looked down at the mass of humanity that filled Fifth Avenue and doubted the sanity of the people. He bemused himself with thoughts of what might be the reaction of a visitor from some other planet. Out in Omaha, reported the *World Herald*, "a young man with a yard of yellow ribbon pinned to the lapel of his box overcoat and armed with a tin horn and a cigaret paraded up and down Farnum Street . . . and had more fun than a box of monkeys with a couple of parrots." When a return for McKinley was posted, "he expanded his cheeks like a bellows and blew the horn until his Adam's apple projected." There were scores of others like him, but "it wasn't all for McKinley, not by a dozen jugs full."

The citizens of San Francisco greeted the news of McKinley's successes in relative calm. Still, someone had set up a steam whistle in front of the *Times* offices, and with every favorable bulletin it produced a blast that could be heard for several blocks. The pool rooms of Denver, all of them equipped to post returns, were crowded to the limit of their capacity. A *Rocky Mountain News* reporter saw there "the men who have been putting up their good money on the election." Yet most of the propositions were called off early; "odds on McKinley went up to ten to one with only an occasional taker." Down in Atlanta, the *Constitution* observed that "it was apparent early in the evening that McKinley was making a sweep of the country." Nevertheless, the throng that braved the steady downpour of rain—and it was predominantly a Bryan crowd—remained until late at night. "Now and then an encouraging report from some part of Georgia would come in to lighten up the monotonous Republican returns. This would be met with a wild yell from the crowd."

There was no shouting or cheering around the Bryan household in Lincoln, however, as the champion of silver read those same monotonous results coming in to the little room where three telegraph operators were kept busy most of the night. For hours he sat there. He wore a black velvet jacket and a pink carnation was stuck in his buttonhole, but to James Creelman he seemed like "a General reading the reports of some great battle in which whole armies were swept away." His eye never changed; the expression on his face was unreadable. As Mrs. Bryan watched him, she could not hide her grief. "It is a terrible thing to look upon a strong man in the pride of youth and see him gather up in his hands the ashes of a great ambition," wrote Creelman, "to watch his face, and know that he is summoning up all the strength of his nature to suppress alternate agony and joy." Finally Bryan went upstairs and stretched himself out on his bed.

Long years later he told his friend, Louis F. Post, that the news of his defeat was a great relief. Before the final reports were in, he said, he had prayed literally and sincerely, "O Lord, let this responsibility be averted; nevertheless not my will but thine be done." When it was all over, Bryan recalled, "I went to bed happy." Yet he did not look very happy when Creelman saw him that night. He refused to concede until the following afternoon, even though he knew that McKinley had been elected. "He uttered no sound of despair," wrote the newspaperman. "But before the end came his face was the face of an old man."

The scene in Canton, meanwhile, was understandably different.

During the afternoon people had begun to crowd onto the McKinley front lawn, or rather what had once been a lawn but was now virtually devoid of grass. The Major ate dinner at six with members of his family. It was a quiet affair. Mrs. McKinley, who had borne the stress of the campaign remarkably well for one in her health, was not quite up to the tensions of the moment and had retired to her room. Later in the evening, however, she joined the other ladies in the dining room, while her husband sat in his library reading returns in the company of his closest friends. Frequently he would go in to his wife and whisper a few words about his impending victory.

Outside the house excitement increased as the crowd grew steadily larger. By midnight the din was terrific. "The sound of factory whistles mingles with a nearer blast of tin horns," wrote reporter William Shaw Bowen. "Some one has erected a megaphone on a lot near by, and from the wide nozzle comes the hoarse tones that suggest those of a fog horn, inquiring: 'What is the matter with McKinley?' Pandemonium is let loose. Canton is beside itself with joy." The Major remarked quietly to one of his companions that he felt the need of rest, but he said that his voice was in good condition and that he had not suffered any real annoyance. "This has been a campaign of oratory, you know," he added with a smile.

An hour later the tumult on Market Street continued unabated. Men at the factories had tied down the levers of steam whistles. Bowen could hardly hear himself think. "The roar of huge sirens and the shriller shrieks of the whistles are rivaled by the clamor of the mob. Red fire is blazing about the house, the grounds are packed with eager people, and points of vantage in the trees are filled with shouting boys." Those who doubted that the volume of sound could be increased had their doubts allayed when McKinley came out on the porch to wave and bow to the multitude. He did not try to speak; he could not have made himself heard. Smiling, he went back inside. Then came the news from Chicago that Chairman Jones refused to concede. It was greeted with jeers and laughter, but with the announcement the crowd began to break up. Tired and happy, the people returned home to rest in the knowledge that the Republic had been saved.

How had it been done? A reporter had asked Mark Hanna that question earlier in the day. The manager had come down to Canton from Cleveland in the afternoon to spend an hour or so with the Major in his library. Jaunty and exuberant, Hanna had responded with confidence. "I have kept them moving, kept them moving all the while. I have not given them a moment's rest." He said that the Democratic National Committee had planned to center its campaign on Michigan, Minnesota, and Indiana, the middle western states where they thought they had the best chance. The Republican organization, without relaxing its efforts in the Middle West, had met the threat by diversionary tactics in the states of the upper South. "I have kept the ball moving in the outlying states at such a lively pace as to require all the energies of our friends, the enemy, to be shown in them," said Hanna. "I have run the campaign as nearly as possible on business principles, and of course I shall be glad if my efforts meet with the approbation of my party." Republicans cheerfully granted their approval as GOP newspapers proclaimed a landslide victory.

Those who had supported the Democratic ticket could not, of course, accept Hanna's analysis. "The battle is over and we have lost!" wrote Arthur Sewall to Bryan. "You have made a noble fight for the principles of our party, but with the press, pulpit and money power against us, the odds were too great." He thought that six months had been too short a time properly to educate the people on the issues. But principles can never die, and Sewall looked forward to victory in four years. John Peter Altgeld was "satisfied that there never again can be the same concentration of adverse conditions and forces that existed this year." He was convinced that another assault on the "fortified strongholds of plutocracy and corruption" would batter them down and drive the money power from the land. A month after the election Altgeld wrote Chairman Jones expressing the belief that "there were fully 100,000 fraudulent votes counted in Illinois this fall," and that "the states of Indiana, Kentucky and California were stolen."

The charges of fraud were coupled with charges of coercion. Mirabeau Towns, Chairman of the Bryan-Sewall Club of Brooklyn, was only one of many who wrote Bryan about tyrannical measures which had been employed against him. "Social ostracism, bank intimidation, employers bulldozing employees and newspaper scurrility and abuse, all combined to one end, had a powerful influence upon the weak and vacillating members of the community." Towns believed that the mid-summer advance in the price of wheat had also had a decisive influence. But even this was not enough fully to account for the defeat of the Democracy. As an easterner, Towns was well aware of the political capital Republicans had made of some of Bryan's radical support. Altgeld, in particular, had been portrayed as the evil influence behind the ticket, and while no one could question his great talents, "his prominence injured our case."

From a Populist viewpoint the failure in November could be attributed to the difficulties of working harmoniously with Democrats. "We ought never to make this kind of campaign again," wrote George F. Washburn, Chairman of the People's party headquarters in Chicago. "The populists cannot continue as an annex or ally, working at cross purposes. We must be merged into one main army, equally recognized and respected." That other members of his party would agree to merge except under Populist leadership may be doubted. "I fear the two elements in our party which have been contending for supremacy, will clash in the near future," commented H. E. Taubeneck. "I am more discouraged over that than any other one thing." Unquestionably divisions in the Bryan camp worked to his disadvantage, and the bolt of gold Democrats did not help matters.

Populists could argue with some justification that they had provided Bryan's most effective support. Yet their discussion of reorganizing under new leadership to advance old causes enunciated in the Omaha platform had a hollow ring. It was Ignatius Donnelly who perhaps best expressed the mood of Populists after the election

"Alas and Alack!" he wrote in his diary after watching the discouraging returns come in. "It seems useless to contend against the money power. Every election marks another step downward into the abyss, from which there will be no return save by fire and sword." Bryan's defeat moved him deeply and stirred doubts about some of his profoundest convictions. "The people are too shallow and too corrupt to conduct a republic," Donnelly wrote on, pouring out his feelings. "It will need a god come on earth with divine power, to save them. And are they worth saving? Will they stay saved?" Unlike Altgeld, he believed the times had never been more favorable or conditions more promising. "We had a splendid candidate and he had made a gigantic campaign; the elements of reform were fairly united; and the depression of business universal, and yet in spite of it all the bankrupt millions voted to keep the yoke on their own necks! I tremble for the future." Then came a wail of anguish: "Will the long lane never have a turning? Will the sun of triumph never rise? I fear not."

If Populists could not hope for better things, however, Democrats were persuaded that they could. They began to play with election figures; and the more they juggled the returns, the more convinced they became that victory would be achieved in 1900. Bryan published a collection of campaign documents, observations, and reminiscences which he entitled, significantly, *The First Battle*. In that work he pointed out that his vote of some 6,500,000 had nearly equaled the combined Democratic and Populist vote in 1892 and had exceeded by almost a million Cleveland's popular vote in 1892. Bryan calculated that his popular vote in the states he carried was 2,427,172, or 829,712 more than the Democratic vote in those states in 1892 and 59,647 more than the vote for both Cleveland and Weaver. In the states which went to McKinley, Bryan's figures indicated that his popular vote was 4,019,294, or 56,069 more than the vote for Cleveland and 214,474 less than the vote for both Cleveland and Weaver. Bryan's vote fell below Cleveland's vote in Alabama, Connecticut, Delaware, Georgia, Louisiana, Maine, Maryland, Massachusetts, New Hampshire, New Jersey, New York, Pennsylvania, Rhode Island, Vermont, Virginia, and Wisconsin. In all other states he ran ahead of the man who sat in the White House from 1893 to 1897.

Bryan did not, however, deal only in facts. He was much too intrigued with what might have been. McKinley's plurality, he observed, was less than the plurality provided by three states: Pennsylvania, New York, and Massachusetts. But what wonders might be accomplished through artful manipulation Bryan was to show when he took a careful look at six closely contested states. He figured that a change of 962 votes in California, 1,059 in Oregon, 142 in Kentucky, 9,002 in Indiana, 2,826 in North Dakota, and 5,445 in West Virginia would have brought him a total of 224 electoral votes and the election. "This calculation," he explained, "is made to show how narrow was the defeat of bimetallism and what is possible for the future." He might have added that the gold Democratic vote in California and Kentucky would have given him those two states.

If McKinley's victory was not as overwhelming as his managers made it out to be, neither was it as close as Bryan would have had it appear. A more impartial analysis than either provided shows that it was neither a landslide nor a hairline victory. Other generalizations can be derived from the accompanying tables. New England, as everyone knew it would, gave McKinley a large majority. He polled more than two-thirds of the votes cast there. Of the three Middle Atlantic States, Cleveland had carried New York and New Jersey in 1892. Bryan lost all three by a combined total of more than 650,000 popular votes. In the five states of the Old Northwest—the crucial section—McKinley polled 2,018,508 votes to Bryan's 1,650,210, and he secured the electoral votes of all five. Cleveland had done much better: Indiana, Illinois, and Wisconsin had given him 51 electoral votes, and he had added 5 more from Michigan and 1 from Ohio.

In the states bordering the northeastern quarter of the country (those Hanna referred to as the "outlying states") McKinley won some important victories. He captured Delaware, Maryland, West Virginia, Iowa, Minnesota, North Dakota, and all but 1 electoral vote in Kentucky. Of those states, only Iowa and Minnesota had voted for Harrison as opposed to Cleveland. McKinley's triumphs in the border and West North Central States could not be described as crushing or overwhelming, but except in Kentucky they were relatively safe ones. They provided him with 54 valuable electoral votes. He could afford to let Bryan sweep the rest of the country, although he did in fact win majorities in Oregon and California.

Just as significant as conclusions that might be drawn from comparing Bryan's showing with that of Cleveland is the long-range trend which the election of 1896 points up. Traditionally, the GOP had been strong in western states, and the South had been solidly Democratic; in the Northeast and the Middle West the parties had been in equilibrium. Elections had gone to Republicans or Democrats as the northeastern quarter of the nation had veered toward one party or the other. One of the most far-reaching political realignments in American history began in 1894, however, when Republicans won heavy majorities throughout most of the country. Until 1912 they were to retain control over every one of the fourteen northeastern states, along with Delaware, Maryland, West Virginia, Iowa, Minnesota, North Dakota, Oregon, and California. In other words, they continued to hold until the election of Woodrow Wilson every state, except Kentucky, that went to McKinley in 1896. Thus for a period of almost twenty years (and they were years of more than passing importance) the GOP dominated that section of the country where industrialization and urbanization were most highly developed. After Wilson there was of course another period of Republican supremacy which lasted until 1932.

Outside the solid South, which was obviously a special case, no such long-range party hegemony is discernible in the states that voted for Bryan. Utah went solidly Republican in the presidential elections after 1896. Kansas, South Dakota, Wyoming, and Washington gave their electoral votes to Republican candidates in 1900, 1904, and 1908. Bryan's own state voted Republican in 1900 and

THE POPULAR VOTE IN 1896

State	Repub-lican	Democrat Populist	National Democrat	Prohibi-tion	Socialist Labor	Total
Alabama	54,737	131,226	6,464	2,147	....	194,574
Arkansas	37,512	110,103	....	893	....	148,508
California	146,688	144,618	2,006	2,573	1,611	297,496
Colorado	26,279	161,269	1	2,110	160	189,819
Connecticut	110,297	56,740	4,336	1,806	1,223	174,402
Delaware	16,883	13,425	887	353	....	31,548
Florida	11,288	32,736	1,778	654	....	46,456
Georgia	60,107	94,733	2,809	5,613	....	163,262
Idaho	6,314	23,135	....	172	....	29,621
Illinois	607,130	464,523	6,390	9,818	1,147	1,089,008
Indiana	323,754	305,573	2,145	5,323	329	637,124
Iowa	289,293	223,741	4,586	3,544	453	521,617
Kansas	159,345	172,915	1,209	2,318	....	335,787
Kentucky	218,171	217,890	5,114	4,781	....	445,956
Louisiana	22,037	77,175	1,834	....	....	101,046
Maine	80,461	34,587	1,867	1,589	....	118,504
Maryland	136,978	104,746	2,507	6,058	588	250,877
Massachusetts	278,976	121,385	11,809	3,060	2,137	417,367
Michigan	293,582	237,268	6,968	6,846	294	544,958
Minnesota	193,503	139,735	....	4,348	954	338,540
Mississippi	5,123	63,793	1,071	485	....	70,472
Missouri	239,333	313,576	2,363	2,462	595	558,329
Montana	10,494	42,537	....	186	....	53,217
Nebraska	103,064	115,999	2,885	2,040	186	224,174
Nevada	1,938	8,376	....	....	....	10,314
New Hampshire	57,444	21,650	3,420	825	228	83,567
New Jersey	221,371	133,695	6,378	5,617	3,986	371,047
New York	819,838	551,513	18,972	16,086	17,731	1,424,140
North Carolina	155,243	174,488	578	681	....	330,990
North Dakota	26,335	20,686	....	358	....	47,379
Ohio	525,991	477,497	1,858	7,784	1,165	1,014,295
Oregon	48,779	46,739	977	919	....	97,414
Pennsylvania	728,300	433,228	11,000	20,147	1,683	1,194,358
Rhode Island	37,437	14,459	1,166	1,161	558	54,781
South Carolina	9,313	58,801	824	....	....	68,938
South Dakota	41,042	41,225	....	683	....	82,950
Tennessee	149,703	168,847	2,106	3,140	....	323,796
Texas	158,894	361,224	4,853	1,722	....	526,693
Utah	13,491	64,607	21	....	....	78,119
Vermont	51,127	10,640	1,331	733	....	63,831
Virginia	135,388	154,985	2,127	2,344	115	294,959
Washington	39,153	51,646	1,668	1,116	....	93,583
West Virginia	105,379	94,488	678	1,223	....	201,768
Wisconsin	268,051	165,349	4,553	7,799	1,311	447,063
Wyoming	10,072	10,375	....	159	....	20,606
Total	7,035,638	6,467,946	131,529	141,676	36,454	13,813,243

Source: House Document 960, *Statistical Abstract of the United States, 1912*, 62d Cong., 3rd Sess., p. 729.

THE ELECTORAL VOTE

Electoral Votes	*and States*	*For President*		*For Vice President*		
		McKinley	Bryan	Hobart	Sewall	Watson
11	Alabama	..	11	..	11	..
8	Arkansas	..	8	..	5	3
9	California	8	1	8	1	..
4	Colorado	..	4	..	4	..
6	Connecticut	6	..	6	..	..
3	Delaware	3	..	3	..	..
4	Florida	..	4	..	4	..
13	Georgia	..	13	..	13	..
3	Idaho	..	3	..	3	..
24	Illinois	24	..	24	..	..
15	Indiana	15	..	15	..	..
13	Iowa	13	..	13	..	..
10	Kansas	..	10	..	10	..
13	Kentucky	12	1	12	1	..
8	Louisiana	..	8	..	4	4
6	Maine	6	..	6	..	..
8	Maryland	8	..	8	..	..
15	Massachusetts	15	..	15	..	..
14	Michigan	14	..	14	..	..
9	Minnesota	9	..	9	..	..
9	Mississippi	..	9	..	9	..
17	Missouri	..	17	..	13	4
3	Montana	..	3	..	2	1
8	Nebraska	..	8	..	4	4
3	Nevada	..	3	..	3	..
4	New Hampshire	4	..	4	..	..
10	New Jersey	10	..	10	..	..
36	New York	36	..	36	..	..
11	North Carolina	..	11	..	6	5
3	North Dakota	3	..	3	..	..
23	Ohio	23	..	23	..	..
4	Oregon	4	..	4	..	..
32	Pennsylvania	32	..	32	..	..
4	Rhode Island	4	..	4	..	..
9	South Carolina	..	9	..	9	..
4	South Dakota	..	4	..	2	2
12	Tennessee	..	12	..	12	..
15	Texas	..	15	..	15	..
3	Utah	..	3	..	2	1
4	Vermont	4	..	4	..	..
12	Virginia	..	12	..	12	..
4	Washington	..	4	..	2	2
6	West Virginia	6	..	6	..	..
12	Wisconsin	12	..	12	..	..
3	Wyoming	..	3	..	2	1
447		271	176	271	149	27

SOURCE: *Congressional Record*, vol. XXIX, pt. 2, 54th Cong., 2d Sess., p. 1694.

1904. The GOP captured Missouri, Montana, and Idaho in 1904 and 1908. And the silver states of Colorado and Nevada went Republican in 1904. The South's consistent record in voting the Democratic ticket had, as in other periods, little to do with anything but a desire to maintain white supremacy.

Analysis of electoral votes and popular votes by states and sections obviously does not disclose everything one might wish to know about voting patterns in 1896. What, for example, was the difference between farm votes and city votes within those states and sections? William Diamond provided an answer to that question in a study published in 1941. By his definition "all agglomerated populations of 45,000 or more" were called "urban." Of the thirty-two states with such concentrations, twenty went to McKinley and twelve to Bryan. The twenty McKinley states contained sixty-five cities, but there were only seventeen cities in the twelve Bryan states. Ten Bryan states had no urban populations at all; three McKinley states had none.

"In the nation as a whole," noted Diamond, "Bryan polled a considerably smaller percentage of the votes of cities than he did of rural sections." This generalization is true of states carried by Bryan as well as of states that went to McKinley. Yet there were some significant differences between the urban vote of Republican states and the urban vote of Democratic states. Relative to his rural vote, Bryan fared better in the cities of northeastern sections and of mineral areas than he did in the cities of southern and western agricultural regions. Cities in New England and in the Mountain States actually gave him a larger percentage of their vote than did the surrounding countryside. Rounding off Diamond's figures, 33½ per cent of the urban and 24½ per cent of the rural vote of New England went to Bryan. In the Mountain States he polled 87 per cent of the urban vote and 80 per cent of the rural. Those were the only sections where his percentage of the urban vote was greater than his percentage of the rural vote.

In the Middle Atlantic States Bryan secured slightly more than 37 per cent of the urban vote and 37⅔ per cent of the rural vote, while in the East North Central States his percentages were 42½ and 44⅔. Cities of New York, however, voted more like those of New England than they did like those of Pennsylvania. Seven of New York's eight cities gave Bryan a higher percentage of votes than did rural portions of the state. Five of the eight cities in Pennsylvania—including the three largest, Philadelphia, Pittsburgh, and Allegheny—gave strong support to McKinley.

"For the remainder of the nation," Diamond observed, "whether one moves westward into the main field of action of the Populists or southward into traditionally Democratic territory, the rural sections of the great majority of the states voted more heavily for Bryan than did the cities located in those states . . . ." Milwaukee, Peoria, and Fort Wayne were alone among cities of the east north central region in giving Bryan a larger percentage of the vote than he received from neighboring rural populations. The silver-tongued orator carried Missouri, Kansas, and Nebraska. But St. Joseph, St. Louis, Omaha, and the two Kansas Cities all gave majorities to McKinley. Nowhere in the nation was the difference between city and country so great as in the South. In that section Bryan received more than 59 per cent of the rural vote but less than 44½ per cent of the urban vote. He lost Kentucky in part because Louisville gave McKinley a heavy majority. Out on the Pacific Coast Portland followed the Louisville pattern.

Totals for the entire country indicate that Bryan secured 40.61 per cent of the urban vote and 48.34 per cent of the rural vote. Of course the urban vote is itself made up of many different elements. Big businessmen and small businessmen, managers and mechanics, skilled workers and unskilled workers, professionals and preachers, ethnic groups and native American groups all contribute to the urban vote. Much investigation must be carried on before anyone can say with certainty which of those groups, if any, were most inclined to cast ballots for McKinley in 1896. Yet discounting the charges of coercion and intimidation, and lacking complete evidence, historians are no doubt justified in concluding that Bryan's program simply did not attract enough votes from urban labor. Bryan necessarily argued economic theory. Anyone who has grappled with the silver issue—or who has tried to explain it to students—can readily understand that McKinley had much the easier task when he could bypass theories and assert that silver meant wages paid in fifty-three cent dollars.

If workers were in general persuaded by Republican arguments, ethnic groups should also have found them convincing. Immigrants probably had difficulty in following Bryan's reasoning, especially when he cast his discussion of the silver question in Jeffersonian or Jacksonian terms. Obviously ethnic groups did not have identical interests, and they were divided in their political loyalties. Bloc voting tended to split the so-called foreign vote even though there were some changes over previous years. According to a careful study of election returns in Chicago, Bryan carried traditionally Democratic Irish and Polish precincts, while McKinley won in Italian, German, and Swedish precincts. Both parties directed appeals, often in the native tongue, to specific ethnic groups. Nevertheless bloc voting can easily be overemphasized; the overriding issues were economic, not ethnic. The depression and the way in which Republicans played upon the prosperity theme help to explain why the Democratic candidate of 1896 received a smaller percentage of the immigrant vote than did the Democratic candidate of 1892.

Bryan's support, then, was primarily rural. But here too it should be pointed out that there was really no such thing as a farm vote per se. Diamond's statistics indicate that, in the various sections, Bryan received from 33.47 to 46.04 per cent of the urban vote. On the other hand his vote in rural areas varied from 24.44 to 59.08 per cent, a much wider range than in the cities. The sectional differences among farmers may be attributed to a number of factors: the degree to which agriculture was diversified, the proportion of farm ownership and tenancy, or the size and distribution of debts and mortgages. Whatever influences may have been in operation Bryan made a poor showing in some agricultural regions. New England farmers gave him a smaller percentage of their ballots than he received from any other rural area. And in the Old Northwest, where one might well argue that he lost the election, he received less than 45 per cent of the rural vote, certainly not a figure he could point to with pride. In Minnesota, one of the states where Democrats thought they had a good chance, Bryan's 40.65 per cent of the farm vote was actually less than his percentage of the urban vote.

If all farmers and workers had agreed on objectives and had considered Bryan's election the only means of achieving them, Ignatius Donnelly would have been right when he said that the American people voted to keep the yoke on their necks. But only masochists would vote for the yoke, and nobody ever won an election by appealing to masochists. The fact is that farmers and workers could not concur on objectives, and failing to unite on goals they failed to unite in support of Bryan or anyone else. The one thing on which all farmers and workers could agree was the truism that they would be better off under conditions of full employment and general economic prosperity. The Republican candidate was widely hailed as the advance agent of prosperity, and he succeeded in persuading voters that the epithet fit.

"The effect of the election was magical in its restoration of commercial confidence," reported *The Review of Reviews* in December. "Buying and selling were immediately resumed, and the demand for goods of all kinds led to the opening of hundreds of factories which had been shut down for a considerable time." The announcement of recovery was premature, but the President-elect came to be regarded as a major economic prophet even before his inauguration. Production curves and indices of business activity began to rise during the summer of 1897. They continued to rise throughout his years in office, and the full dinner pail became McKinley's symbol. By 1900 people wondered what all the shouting had been about.

Bryan tried to explain. Principles were eternal. What was true in 1896 would always be true, and he refused to budge from the position he had taken. He insisted that the Democracy write a silver plank into its platform in 1900. Many thought at the time that he was both stubborn and fatuous; many more have continued to think so ever since. But that does not mean he was wrong. On the contrary, he always maintained that he had been right. He had pleaded for an increase in the money supply through the free coinage of silver. Even though a free coinage law was never passed, money stock did increase rapidly after 1896. Its growth was interrupted only once during the period of Republican ascendency which began with McKinley's election. New gold discoveries in Alaska, Australia, and South Africa, as well as the cyanide process, helped to bring about that result. World output of gold increased from an average of some 5 or 6 million ounces annually to 22 million ounces by 1910.

During the campaign of 1900 Bryan contended that not enough gold had yet been released to produce the desired result and that free coinage would still be beneficial. Not until 1907, seven years after Congress had passed a gold standard act, did he concede that free silver was no longer necessary. Whatever justification he might have had for insisting that he had been right in principle, his continued appeals for silver fell on skeptical ears. Compared with McKinley, Bryan sounded like a faker. He seemed even more foolish and misguided than Grover Cleveland. From that day to this Republicans have been prone to characterize the Democratic party as the party of economic vagaries and fiscal irresponsibility.

Although Bryan emphasized silver as the paramount issue in 1896, his harp had more than one string. From the beginning of his active political career he argued that parties had a responsibility to frame issues and explain them to the people. A new issue—the issue of imperialism—arose during the McKinley years. Industrialists and administration men began to assert with increasing conviction that, as Theodore C. Search, President of the National Association of Manufacturers, put it, "Manufacturers have found the capacity of the home market insufficient to absorb their normal output, and the only avenue of relief has presented itself in an enlarged export trade." The belief that industrialization had proceeded faster than the power of the home market to consume provided a motive for McKinley's program of expansion. To his mind, military victories in the Spanish-American War justified acquisition of Puerto Rico, Guam, and the Philippines. But beyond that, establishing control over the islands was essentially a move toward finding new markets overseas. The Open Door policy in China grew out of the same considerations. Imperialists applauded McKinley's line of action, whether they recognized its economic implications or not; it was a mark of the nation's greatness and a sure sign of its future importance in world affairs.

Bryan, on the other hand, fought the new interpretation of manifest destiny with all the eloquence at his command. Instead of developing markets overseas, he proposed to raise general American purchasing power to the point where American production could be absorbed in markets at home. During the debate over imperialism he played the part of opposition leader, a role he assumed naturally after 1896. A persistent critic of both foreign and domestic policies which the national government pursued during the years of Republican ascendency, he was to serve his country well. Long after McKinley lay dead at the hands of a demented assassin, Bryan was a force of major importance in American politics.

Having won fame and a loyal following in 1896, he used both in urging a variety of causes and reforms: tariff reform, an income tax, trust regulation, a guarantee of bank deposits, abandonment of the injunction as a weapon in labor disputes, reform of rules in the House of Representatives, the direct election of senators, woman suffrage, the initiative, referendum, and recall, direct primaries, and international arbitration. In 1906 he also came out for government ownership of railroads, although he soon abandoned the idea on grounds that the American people were not yet ready for it. Later on he began to agitate for prohibition. For the most part he was consistent in his demands and at the same time acutely conscious of a need to adapt programs and policies to fluctuating conditions. He was in some measure responsible for the successes of the progressive period. One may well argue that his contribution was as important as any he might have made had he been elected in 1896, or in 1900 when he ran again, or in 1908 when he was defeated for the third and last time.

Part of the importance of the election of 1896—and perhaps the chief reason for its fascination—lies in the insight into American politics which it affords. Seers of the time commonly saw signs that pointed to revolution, or at the very least to radical innovations. The depression of the nineties increased the intensity of labor unrest and agrarian discontent. Some welcomed the indications of upheaval, while others feared them. But politics and parties functioned in such a way as to thwart a revolutionary thrust. The sword of radicalism was broken before it could strike a blow. The limited character of Bryan's monetary reforms assured the continuity of American political and economic development regardless of the outcome at the polls.

To conservatives, then, the election of 1896 provides an outstanding example of what one of them has called "the genius of American politics." This "genius" involves nothing more and nothing less than a capacity to consider and dispose of concrete issues without resorting to doctrinaire and revolutionary extremes. Never dogmatic, it has taken the American experience as its guide. Thus it has sometimes found expression in myths which that experience has appeared to validate. So it was with the myth of the self-made man and the myth of the yeoman which shaped the thinking of McKinley and Bryan.

To those of more radical temperament, the election demonstrates what they feel is becoming increasingly obvious in the second half of the twentieth century: that parties and political institutions are structurally inadequate and that they are incapable of responding to changing economic and social needs. Among other things, critics have pointed to shortcomings of legislative processes, to conflicts of interest between state and national governments, to weaknesses in the instruments of economic control, to crippling disagreements on the role of the national government in areas of social welfare, education, and civil rights. Back in the 1890's, many Populists shared

Bryan's belief in the agrarian myth; many workers entertained thoughts of becoming self-made men. But the truly radical thinkers, those for whom Henry Demarest Lloyd spoke, recognized the myths for what they were and sought to face the economic realities of that period.

Both Bryan and McKinley, each in his own way, took the side of the conservatives. Perhaps they sensed that radicalism might itself produce rigidities which could prevent all hope of realizing the American dream. But that is unlikely, for neither one contemplated reaching a final utopia. Certainly they could not have foreseen that in the frustration of defeat some of the most disappointed of Populists would create a terrifying mystique based on nativism, negrophobia, and growing convictions that honest folk were victims of a nefarious conspiracy.

While acceptance of traditional myths influenced Bryan and McKinley in their perception of realities, it did not necessarily make them blind to fundamental questions. William Jennings Bryan went to the heart of the political struggle of the nineties in his "Cross of Gold" speech: "changing conditions make new issues; . . . the principles upon which Democracy rests are as everlasting as the hills, but . . . they must be applied to new conditions as they arise." He was touching on what would become the central problem facing Americans in the twentieth century, the problem of advancing and applying democratic principles in a period when social, economic, and technological changes were more rapid and far-reaching than ever before.

Bibliographical Essay

THIS ESSAY is concerned with books and references which may be found in good libraries or are otherwise readily available. It makes no mention of manuscript collections and other sources which have been consulted in the preparation of this volume, but which are of interest chiefly to specialists.

Several general works on American thought and society provide a basis for understanding the social and intellectual backgrounds of the election of 1896. Ralph Gabriel, *The Course of American Democratic Thought* (New York: The Ronald Press Company, 1956) is a study in continuity, tracing the development of the American democratic faith from 1815 to the present. Stow Persons, *American Minds* (New York: Holt, Rinehart and Winston, Inc., 1958) takes a different approach in identifying dominant thought patterns with various periods. His chapters on the "naturalistic mind" are particularly useful for the student of the late nineteenth century. Another basic study of American thought since the 1890's is Henry Steele Commager's *The American Mind* (New Haven: Yale University Press, 1950). Daniel Boorstin, *The Genius of American Politics* (Chicago: The University of Chicago Press, 1953) is brief but suggestive. Important aspects of social history are covered in Arthur M. Schlesinger, Jr., *The Rise of the City, 1878-1898* (New York: The Macmillan Company, 1933). Eric Goldman's *Rendezvous With Destiny* (New York: Alfred A. Knopf, 1953) is a well-written survey of American reform movements since the Civil War. A systematic survey of American economic thought may be found in Joseph Dorfman, *The Economic Mind in American Civilization,* vol. III (New York: The Viking Press, Inc., 1949). Contemporary periodicals, especially *The Review of Reviews, Public Opinion,* and *The Literary Digest,* are indispensable sources of information.

Recent scholarship has done much to clarify the myths by which nineteenth-century Americans lived. For analysis of the agrarian point of view see A. Whitney Griswold, *Farming and Democracy* (New York: Harcourt, Brace and Company, Inc., 1948); Henry Nash Smith, *Virgin Land* (Cambridge: Harvard University Press, 1950); and Richard Hofstadter, *The Age of Reform, From Bryan to F.D.R.* (New York: Alfred A. Knopf, 1955). Especially useful for Social Darwinism and the myth of the self-made man are Stow Persons, ed., *Evolutionary Thought in America* (New Haven: Yale University Press, 1950); Irwin G. Wyllie, *The Self-Made Man in America* (New Brunswick: Rutgers University Press, 1954); and Richard Hofstadter, *Social Darwinism in American Thought* (Boston: Beacon Press, 1955).

Reference works helpful in the study of the election of 1896 are Richard C. Bain, *Convention Decisions and Voting Records* (Washington, D.C.: The Brookings Institute, 1960); Kirk Porter, ed., *National Party Platforms* (New York: The Macmillan Company, 1924); W. Dean Burnham, *Presidential Ballots, 1824-1892* (Baltimore: The Johns Hopkins Press, 1955); and Edgar Eugene Robinson, *The Presidential Vote, 1896-1932* (Stanford University: Stanford University Press, 1934). Special mention should be made of the U.S. Bureau of the Census, *Historical Statistics of the United States, Colonial Times to 1957* (Washington, D.C.: U.S. Government Printing Office, 1960), which contains a wealth of information.

No balanced and scholarly full-length biography of William Jennings Bryan has yet been published. The first volume of Paolo Coletta's two-volume biography is scheduled to appear in 1964. Paxton Hibben's satirical *The Peerless Leader: William Jennings Bryan* (New York: Farrar & Rinehart, Inc., 1929) is highly readable but unfair. Equally inadequate are M. R. Werner, *Bryan* (New York: Harcourt, Brace and Company, Inc., 1929) and the more sympathetic J. C. Long, *Bryan, The Great Commoner* (New York: D. Appleton & Company, Inc., 1928). W. J. and Mary Bryan, *Memoirs of William Jennings Bryan* (Philadelphia: John C. Winston Company, 1925) is sketchy and incomplete, although it does contain information that cannot be found elsewhere. Various phases of Bryan's life are treated in George R. Poage, "The College Career of William Jennings Bryan," *Mississippi Valley Historical Review*, XV (1928), pp. 165-182; Paolo Coletta, "The Youth of William Jennings Bryan—Beginnings of a Christian Statesman," *Nebraska History*, XXXI (1950), pp. 1-24; and Paul W. Glad, *The Trumpet Soundeth, William Jennings Bryan and His Democracy, 1896-1912* (Lincoln: University of Nebraska Press, 1960).

The best biographies of McKinley are Margaret Leech's *In the Days of*

McKinley (New York: Harper & Brothers, 1959) and H. Wayne Morgan's *William McKinley and His America* (Syracuse: Syracuse University Press, 1963). Charles S. Olcott, *The Life of William McKinley,* 2 vols. (Boston: Houghton Mifflin Company, 1916) is laudatory and of little value except for some details of McKinley's life. For McKinley's financial problems see H. Wayne Morgan, "Governor McKinley's Misfortune: The Walker-McKinley Fund of 1893," *Ohio Historical Quarterly,* LIV (1960), pp. 103-120. The most useful study of Mark Hanna is still Herbert Croly's *Marcus Alonzo Hanna* (New York: The Macmillan Company, 1919). Thomas E. Felt, "The Rise of Mark Hanna" (unpublished Ph.D. dissertation, Michigan State University, 1960) contains new material and is exceptionally well written.

William Allen White's *Autobiography* (New York: The Macmillan Company, 1946) and his *Masks in a Pageant* (New York: The Macmillan Company, 1928) are filled with interesting insights. See also Walter Johnson, *William Allen White's America* (New York: Henry Holt and Company, Inc., 1947). The memoirs of Joseph B. Foraker, *Notes of a Busy Life,* 2 vols. (Cincinnati: Stewart and Kidd Co., 1916) provide some good material on Ohio politics. Among the most valuable biographies of Republican leaders are William A. Robinson, *Thomas B. Reed, Parliamentarian* (New York: Dodd, Mead & Company, Inc., 1930); Leland Sage, *William Boyd Allison* (Iowa City: State Historical Society of Iowa, 1956); and James W. Neilson, *Shelby M. Cullom, Prairie State Republican* (Urbana: University of Illinois Press, 1962). Elmer Ellis, *Henry Moore Teller, Defender of the West* (Caldwell, Idaho: The Caxton Printers, Ltd., 1941) is a good biography of the Silver Republican leader.

On the Democratic side, the autobiographical work of Willis J. Abbot, *Watching the World Go By* (Boston: Little, Brown and Company, 1933) is balanced and moderate. Allan Nevins, *Grover Cleveland, A Study in Courage* (New York: Dodd, Mead & Company, Inc., 1933) is standard but not so critical as Horace S. Merrill's shorter study, *Bourbon Leader: Grover Cleveland and the Democratic Party* (Boston: Little, Brown and Company, 1957). James A. Barnes, *John G. Carlisle, Financial Statesman* (New York: Dodd, Mead & Company, Inc., 1931) is a sympathetic treatment. Other biographies of leading Democrats are Mark Hirsch, *William C. Whitney* (New York: Dodd, Mead & Company, Inc., 1948); Horace S. Merrill, *William Freeman Vilas* (Madison: State Historical Society of Wisconsin, 1954); James C. Olson, *J. Sterling Morton*

(Lincoln: University of Nebraska Press, 1942); Joseph Wall, *Henry Watterson, Reconstructed Rebel* (New York: Oxford University Press, 1956); John R. Lambert, *Arthur Pue Gorman* (Baton Rouge: Louisiana State University Press, 1953); Harry Barnard, *"Eagle Forgotten," The Life of John Peter Altgeld* (Indianapolis: The Bobbs-Merrill Company, 1938); and Ray Ginger, *Altgeld's America; The Lincoln Ideal Versus Changing Realities* (New York: Funk & Wagnalls Company, 1958).

By far the most penetrating biography of a radical or Populist leader is C. Vann Woodward, *Tom Watson, Agrarian Rebel* (New York: The Macmillan Company, 1938). Martin Ridge's *Ignatius Donnelly, The Portrait of a Politician* (Chicago: The University of Chicago Press, 1962) is thorough and contains much new material. Caroline Augusta Lloyd, *Henry Demarest Lloyd*, 2 vols. (New York: G. P. Putnam's Sons, 1918) reproduces some important correspondence, but is partisan. No adequate study of Lloyd has yet been published. For Populism and radicalism see also Frederick E. Haynes, *James Baird Weaver* (Iowa City: The State Historical Society of Iowa, 1919); Francis B. Simkins, *Pitchfork Ben Tillman* (Baton Rouge: Louisiana State University Press, 1941); Ray Ginger, *The Bending Cross; A Biography of Eugene Victor Debs* (New Brunswick: Rutgers University Press, 1949); and H. Wayne Morgan, *Eugene V. Debs; Socialist for President* (Syracuse: Syracuse University Press, 1962).

One of the most interesting and interpretive of the many studies in American politics is Richard Hofstadter's *The American Political Tradition and the Men Who Made It* (New York: Alfred A. Knopf, 1948). Matthew Josephson, *The Politicos, 1865-1896* (New York: Harcourt, Brace and Company, Inc., 1938) is brilliantly written, but sometimes misleading. A survey of American party history may be found in Wilfred E. Binkley, *American Political Parties, Their Natural History* (New York: Alfred A. Knopf, 1945). Harold U. Faulkner, *Politics, Reform, and Expansion, 1890-1900* (New York: Harper & Brothers, 1959) has excellent chapters on the politics of the 1890's. William Jennings Bryan, *The First Battle* (Chicago: W. B. Conkey Company, 1897) contains significant campaign documents. Charles G. Dawes, *A Journal of the McKinley Years* (Chicago: R. R. Donnelley & Sons Company, 1950) is an important source for the McKinley campaign.

Special studies of value are Horace S. Merrill, *Bourbon Democracy of the Middle West, 1865-1896* (Baton Rouge: Louisiana State University

Press, 1953); Francis B. Simkins, *The Tillman Movement in South Carolina* (Durham: Duke University Press, 1926); George Knoles, *The Presidential Campaign and Election of 1892* (Stanford University: Stanford University Press, 1942); and Vincent P. De Santis, *Republicans Face the Southern Question, 1877-1897* (Baltimore: The Johns Hopkins Press, 1959). Joseph Schafer, Jr., "The Presidential Election of 1896" (unpublished Ph.D. dissertation, University of Wisconsin, 1941) has been widely used. A broader investigation is J. Rogers Hollingsworth, *The Whirligig of Politics* (Chicago: University of Chicago Press, 1963). An extended treatment of the election of 1896 by Stanley Jones is scheduled for publication by the University of Wisconsin Press in 1964.

A number of scholarly articles deal with various phases of the election of 1896 and the personalities involved. Among the most important are William Diamond, "Urban and Rural Voting in 1896," *American Historical Review,* XLVI (1941), pp. 281-305; John E. Pixton, Jr., "Charles G. Dawes and the McKinley Campaign," *Journal of the Illinois State Historical Society,* XLVIII (1955), pp. 283-306; Gilbert Fite, "Republican Strategy and the Farm Vote," *American Historical Review,* LXV (1960), pp. 787-806; Elmer Ellis, "Silver Republicans in 1896," *Mississippi Valley Historical Review,* XVIII (1932), pp. 519-534; Jeannette P. Nichols, "Bryan's Benefactor: Coin Harvey and His World," *The Ohio Historical Quarterly,* LXVII (1958), pp. 299-325; Harvey Wish, "John Peter Altgeld and the Background of the Campaign of 1896," *Mississippi Valley Historical Review,* XXIV (1938), pp. 503-518; James A. Barnes, "Myths of the Bryan Campaign," *Mississippi Valley Historical Review,* XXXIV (1947), pp. 367-404; Barnes, "Gold Standard Democrats and Party Conflict," *Mississippi Valley Historical Review,* XVII (1930), pp. 422-450; Paolo Coletta, "William Jennings Bryan and the Nebraska Senatorial Election of 1893," *Nebraska History,* XXXI (1950), pp. 183-203; Coletta, "The Morning Star of the Reformation: William Jennings Bryan's First Congressional Campaign," *Nebraska History,* XXXVII (1956), pp. 103-119; and Coletta, "Bryan, Cleveland, and the Disrupted Democracy," *Nebraska History,* XLI (1960), pp. 1-27.

Populism is a subject of continuing interest in American historiography. The backgrounds of agrarian radicalism are treated in Solon J. Buck, *The Granger Movement* (Cambridge: Harvard University Press, 1913) which is still useful. John D. Hicks, *The Populist Revolt* (Minneapolis: University of Minnesota Press, 1931) and Fred Shannon, *The Farmer's*

Last Frontier (New York: Farrar & Rinehart, Inc. 1945) are basic studies. Theodore Saloutos, *Farmer Movements in the South, 1865-1933* (Berkeley: University of California Press, 1960) provides information on an area neglected by many writers. Two excellent studies which relate indirectly to Populism are Allan Bogue, *Money at Interest, The Farm Mortgage on the Middle Border* (Ithaca: Cornell University Press, 1955), and James C. Malin, *Winter Wheat in the Golden Belt of Kansas* (Lawrence: University of Kansas Press, 1944).

Five highly provocative interpretations of Populism and agrarian radicalism should be considered together. Chester M. Destler's collection of essays, *American Radicalism, 1865-1901* (New London: Connecticut College, 1946), is a pioneering work that retains its freshness. C. Vann Woodward, *Origins of the New South, 1877-1913* (Baton Rouge: Louisiana State University Press, 1951) contains profound insights into the nature of southern Populism. Richard Hofstadter, *The Age of Reform,* mentioned previously, has stimulated much discussion of Populism and reform movements. Norman Pollack, *The Populist Response to Industrial America, Midwestern Populist Thought* (Cambridge: Harvard University Press, 1962) and Walter T. K. Nugent, *The Tolerant Populists* (Chicago: University of Chicago Press, 1963) reject many of Hofstadter's interpretations.

There have been several studies of Populism in the various states. The best are Alex M. Arnett, *The Populist Movement in Georgia* (New York: Columbia University Press, 1922); Roscoe C. Martin, *The People's Party in Texas* (Austin: University of Texas, 1933); and William D. Sheldon, *Populism in the Old Dominion, Virginia Farm Politics, 1885-1900* (Princeton, N.J.: Princeton University Press, 1935). Among the older but still useful pieces on agrarian radicalism are Hallie Farmer, "Economic Background of Frontier Populism," *Mississippi Valley Historical Review,* X (1924), pp. 406-427; John D. Barnhart, "Rainfall and the Populist Party in Nebraska," *American Political Science Review,* XIX (1925), pp. 527-540; Leon W. Fuller, "Colorado's Revolt Against Capitalism," *Mississippi Valley Historical Review,* XXI (1934), pp. 343-360; and Benton H. Wilcox, "An Historical Definition of Northwestern Radicalism," *Mississippi Valley Historical Review,* XXVI (1939), pp. 377-394.

Anyone studying the election of 1896 must necessarily read widely in business and economic history. A good introduction is Thomas C. Cochran and William Miller, *The Age of Enterprise, A Social History of Industrial America* (New York: Harper Torchbooks, 1961). Edward C. Kirkland, *Industry Comes of Age; Business, Labor and Public Policy, 1860-1897* (New York: Holt, Rinehart and Winston, Inc., 1961) is a valuable contribution to "The Economic History of the United States" series, of which it is volume VI. Far less objective is Matthew Josephson, *The Robber Barons; The Great American Capitalists, 1861-1901* (New York: Harcourt, Brace and Company, Inc., 1934).

The classic study of government financial policy is Davis R. Dewey, *Financial History of the United States* (New York: Longmans, Green & Co. Inc., 1956). Fritz Redlich, *The Molding of American Banking: Men and Ideas, Part II, 1840-1910* (New York: Hafner Publishing Company, Inc., 1951) is highly original in conception and approach. The same might be said for Robert P. Sharkey's important study of the Civil War and Reconstruction period, *Money, Class, and Party* (Baltimore: The Johns Hopkins Press, 1959) which interprets developments that formed part of the background of 1896. Victor S. Clark, *History of Manufacturers in the United States, 1607-1914* (Washington, D.C.: Carnegie Institution of Washington, 1916-1928) is a bulky volume which contains a wealth of information on various industries. Edwin Frickey, *Production in the United States, 1860-1914* (Cambridge: Harvard University Press, 1947) provides extensive statistical data. The standard work on labor is John R. Commons, *et al.*, *History of Labor in the United States*, 4 vols. (New York: The Macmillan Company, 1918-1935), but it should be supplemented by Norman Ware, *The Labor Movement in the United States, 1860-1895: A Study in Democracy* (New York: D. Appleton & Company, Inc., 1929). See also Philip Taft, *The A.F. of L. in the Time of Gompers* (New York: Harper & Brothers, 1957) and Almont Lindsey, *The Pullman Strike* (Chicago: The University of Chicago Press, 1942).

A suggestive interpretation of business cycles is Rendigs Fels, *American Business Cycles, 1865-1897* (Chapel Hill: University of North Carolina Press, 1959). The significant findings of Milton Friedman and his associates have been reported in the National Bureau of Economic Research, *Thirty-fifth Annual Report* (New York, 1955); in Friedman, "The Demand for Money," *Journal of Political Economy*, LXVII (1959), pp. 327-351; and in Friedman, *A Program for Monetary Stability* (New York: Fordham University Press, 1959). Charles Hoffmann's "The Depression of the Nineties," *Journal of Economic History*, XVI (1956), pp. 137-164, is a good survey of the subject. Oliver M. W. Sprague, *History of Crises under the National Banking System* (Senate Document 538, 61st Cong., 2d Sess.) has a chapter on the Panic of 1893 which is still useful. Another side of the depression of the nineties is treated in Samuel Rezneck, "Unemployment, Unrest, Relief in the United States during the Depression of 1893-1897," *Journal of Political Economy,* LXI (1953), pp. 324-345. Thomas J. McCormick, "'A Fair Field and No Favor,' American China Policy during the McKinley Administrations, 1897-1901" (unpublished Ph.D. dissertation, University of Wisconsin, 1961) brilliantly and lucidly traces development of the overproduction theory which became important in McKinley's thinking. William Appleman Williams, *The Tragedy of American Diplomacy* (New York: Dell Publishing Company, Inc., 1962) explores with imagination and insight the way in which economic influences shaped the formation of foreign policy.

INDEX

Paul W. Glad is Merrick Professor of History at the University of Oklahoma. Born in Salt Lake City, he studied at Purdue University and Indiana University. His other books include *The Trumpet Soundeth: William Jennings Bryan and His Democracy.*

ELEPHANT PAPERBACKS

American History and American Studies

Stephen Vincent Benét, *John Brown's Body,* EL10
Paul Boyer, ed., *Reagan as President,* EL117
Robert V. Bruce, *1877: Year of Violence,* EL102
George Dangerfield, *The Era of Good Feelings,* EL110
Clarence Darrow, *Verdicts Out of Court,* EL2
Floyd Dell, *Intellectual Vagabondage,* EL13
Elisha P. Douglass, *Rebels and Democrats,* EL108
Theodore Draper, *The Roots of American Communism,* EL105
Joseph Epstein, *Ambition,* EL7
Paul W. Glad, *McKinley, Bryan, and the People,* EL119
Edward Chase Kirkland, *Dream and Thought in the Business Community, 1860–1900,* EL114
Herbert S Klein, *Slavery in the Americas,* EL103
Aileen S. Kraditor, *Means and Ends in American Abolitionism,* EL111
Leonard W. Levy, *Jefferson and Civil Liberties: The Darker Side,* EL107
Seymour J. Mandelbaum, *Boss Tweed's New York,* EL112
Thomas J. McCormick, *China Market,* EL115
Walter Millis, *The Martial Spirit,* EL104
Roderick Nash, *The Nervous Generation,* EL113
William L. O'Neill, ed., *Echoes of Revolt: The Masses, 1911–1917,* EL5
Glenn Porter and Harold C. Livesay, *Merchants and Manufacturers,* EL106
Bernard Sternsher, ed., *Hitting Home: The Great Depression in Town and Country,* EL109
Nicholas von Hoffman, *We Are the People Our Parents Warned Us Against,* EL301
Norman Ware, *The Industrial Worker, 1840–1860,* EL116
Tom Wicker, *JFK and LBJ: The Influence of Personality upon Politics,* EL120
Robert H. Wiebe, *Businessmen and Reform,* EL101
Miles Wolff, *Lunch at the 5 & 10,* EL118